Courtnee,

WHEN GOD ALLOWS THE RAIN

What journey this has been.
Thank you for sharing your
heart with me and everyone
that picks up this book.
Blessings upon blessings
be yours now and always,
 Much Love,

 Dela

WHEN GOD ALLOWS THE RAIN

HOW TO EMBRACE
THE PAIN
AND CELEBRATE HIS PURPOSE!

DR. DELON RADEBAUGH

Published by BookLocker.com, Inc., St. Petersburg, Florida.

Printed on acid-free paper.

BookLocker.com, Inc.
2018

First Edition

Unless otherwise noted, all scripture verses are
from the King James Version.

"Now the God of hope fill you with all joy and peace in believing, that ye may abound in hope, through the power of the Holy Ghost"

(Romans 15:13).

"But thanks *be* to God, which giveth us the victory through our Lord Jesus Christ"

(1 Corinthians 15:57).

SPECIAL THANKS

To God be the glory for the things he has done! I am humbled and honored by his love for me. In every storm of my life, God has pulled me close, comforted me, and even corrected me, all with lovingkindness and mercy.

Keith, Jarred, Jordan, Jonah, and Hannah, we've done it again. Your love and support push me to use my gifts and chase my dreams. You keep me going. I write to inspire you to love God and share that love with everyone you meet. Jonah, you did an awesome job with the layout. You're brilliant!

Pastor Odie Kennedy, you have weathered every storm with grace and dignity. Thank you for being an example of both strength and humility.

To my Godchildren, never give up! Nothing is impossible with God.

To Venita, you have taught me so much! Thank you for your contribution to this book, but more importantly, to my life. Your example, prayers, and love mean the world to me.

To Courtnee, Sharndell, Davida, and Addison, thank you for your willingness to openly share your love, journey, rain, and triumph. You are true superheroes!

To my church family, you're the best!

To my friends, thank you for never allowing me to let go of the promises of God.

To my editors and publishers, thank you for helping me share the word that God has given me. Together, we are placing life in the hands of every reader.

To the person holding this book, thank you for opening your heart. The Lord has brought us together and for that I am grateful. I pray you are strengthened, inspired, and encouraged. Most of all, I pray you are drawn closer to God.

CONTENT

FOREWORD

Integrity is an attribute many struggle to maintain, but Dr. Radebaugh is refining it through her pen. I delight in every opportunity to witness her evolution as a prolific writer and noteworthy author, from her genesis: *A Little Girl's Journey: I Made It!* to *When God Allows the Rain.* Undoubtedly, her latest project will capture us all by teaching us to accept what God allows and count it a privilege to suffer for His sake. I believe her creed follows that which Paul declares in 2 Corinthians 12:9-10 KJV, "And he said unto me, My grace is sufficient for thee: for my strength is made perfect in weakness. Most gladly therefore will I rather glory in my infirmities, that the power of Christ may rest upon me. Therefore I take pleasure in infirmities, in reproaches, in necessities, in persecutions, in distresses for Christ's sake: for when I am weak, then am I strong."

Many people view their past experiences as dark tunnels leading them into an abyss, but Dr. Radebaugh has used her past experiences as a window for opportunities that continue to lead her to limitless possibilities. She sees the world through different lenses, noticing life's intricate details as a kaleidoscope of hues that teach life lessons with a broader spectrum. Dr. Dee speaks truths in realistic, nontraditional fashions. She seizes the truths we all avoid, cultivates the truths we all ignore, and presents the truths we all crave, in engaging and palatable modes.

Dr. Radebaugh is relentless in her quest to present God as a Person, with whom you can have a meaningful relationship; Jesus as a friend, to whom you can tell your innermost secrets; and the Holy Ghost as a companion, on whom you can depend, to be with you, through every situation in your life. Her mission resonates through her personal testimony, "I believe God" and her personal pen. Dr. Delon Radebaugh is a wife, mother, grandmother, godmother, daughter, sister, aunt, friend, entrepreneur, "brand: #Dr. Dee", and, most notably, the most passionate, sincere, and honest woman of God I know.

Evangelist Missionary
Venita L. Thomas-O'Hara

INTRODUCTION

When pain puts its arms around me, I

have the power to control how I

respond. So do you!

Embrace the pain? Celebrate? I used to think that anyone who said anything remotely close to that had to be a lunatic. Why in the world would I welcome pain? Was I looking at the phrase all wrong or at the person all wrong? Or both?

When I was a little girl, I was molested. I can remember hiding in the bathroom with the door locked while my attacker sat on the other side telling me what he was going to do to me. His laugh hurt me almost as much as his hands. It seemed to snake its way under the door. I could practically see his gold toothy smile full of excitement. My eyes would immediately burn when I heard that he was coming over, knowing that soon it would happen again. I wondered why I was his target. Was it because I was small? Because he knew I was too scared to tell anyone? Or just because he knew the truth about me? He knew I wasn't related to him by blood, so I didn't really matter?

Whatever the reason, the pain he inflicted hurt me in places that his hands couldn't touch. I didn't know what to call it then but as I got older, it became clear. He put holes in my soul and kissed my self-worth away. It was a distress that I couldn't describe but could feel even when he wasn't around. Molestation was a rain that doused my spirit. From the first violation, it changed me. On the outside, I tried to act like myself so that no one would figure out my shame. I laughed in front of all the right people, but inside I became dark. My hopefulness faded with every encounter. I cringed at the thought of any physical contact from anyone, even if I really wanted it. My mother wasn't especially affectionate, but I desperately craved her touch. When she reached in my direction, I would practically panic. What if I cried or looked at her wrong? How would she interpret that? I became a worrier. I worried about how I dressed, what I looked like, and what others thought of me. His touch changed the way I saw myself. That rain lasted well into adulthood.

Later I was told I should embrace that pain as a way to cope. What does that even mean? What was I being asked to do? It took years of reflection, discovery, and prayer to deal with the torment. When I think of the word *embrace*, I think of hugging. When people reach out to hug me, I can take them into my bosom, which means bringing them into my heart, or I can half-heartedly hug them back just for the sake of keeping the peace. Another choice is to allow them to hug me but to keep my arms at my side. No doubt this says I am uninterested in what you are offering and not reciprocating. Or I can shove them so hard that they fall flat on their hug! All of this puts *me* in control of the situation. Being able to choose my reaction empowers me. All of these are more than just options, they are decisions. I have the power to control how I respond when pain puts its arms around me. So do you!

Now I'm not saying that embracing your pain will feel good or you will like it. To be honest, it makes me think of hugging a pole full of knives that you know are going to cut you to pieces. Hugging it sounds ridiculous and, yes, maybe it is, but hugging that pole can take you from victim to conqueror. You need to face your fear and for that you need the mindset of a conqueror. To embrace your pain means to approach it in a way that helps you win. You *use it* instead of letting it use you. Embracing doesn't mean that you like what has been done to you, but that you are welcoming the lessons it can teach. Pain can be empowering if your perspective will allow it. It can suffocate or motivate. It's up to you.

I never accepted being molested. It never should have happened. Nothing I do today will undo what happened, but I can do something now. I can thank God for bringing me through the storm. "What!?" you may ask. "Why are you not asking God why he let it happen in the first place?" Believe me, I wondered that. I grew up believing in God *and* that bad things happen to good people. Not because God doesn't care, but because people don't. They do what they want and think that they'll never have to answer for it.

Could it be that there was purpose in my pain? Over the course of my adult life, I have had the opportunity to look little girls in the eye and be real with them. I have shared my story in schools, churches, and even on the bus. In those moments, I don't share only the dark pain of my experience, but I share what I'm doing with it now. I don't share only what my abuser took from me, but what God allowed me to gain by the experience. Every time I share it, I dull the tips of those knives. I dull the shame. It was not my fault, but it is *my* story. I own it!

Every time I share my story, it isn't full of happy quotes. Sometimes there are lots of tears and heartache. I still hurt when I think of what I went through but, ultimately, I celebrate. "What is there to celebrate?" I'm glad you asked. I celebrate that I didn't lie there and die. I didn't give up on it stopping. Somehow, I knew it couldn't last forever. I celebrate that I could trust God to take care of me and I could still believe in His love for me. I celebrate that I stopped seeing myself through the molester's eyes and started seeing myself through God's eyes. I wasn't powerless, but more than a conqueror. I learned to embrace my pain and celebrate God's purpose!

Don't think this happened overnight. It happened over nights of crying and wishing it would all go away. It happened over years of learning more about God and who he is. I finally had to decide to embrace my pain to take away its power.

In this book, you will find others who are willing to share their rain and how God has delivered them. Their honesty and hope are the result of their intimate relationship with God.

As you delve into the rain that God has allowed in your life, know that you are neither hopeless nor powerless. You have the power and authority to overcome when you finally decide to do so. When you make your mind up that you will let God help you through the storm, you will see his hand at work.

As we begin this book, there must be a couple of ground rules:

First, **God exist**. "For without faith *it is* impossible to please *him*: for he that cometh to God must believe that he is, and *that* he is a rewarder of them that diligently seek him" (Hebrews 11:6).

Second, **Jesus is Alive**. "That if thou shalt confess with thy mouth the Lord Jesus, and shalt believe in thine heart that God hath raised him from the dead, thou shalt be saved" (Romans 10:9).

Nothing in this book will help you without believing that God exist and Jesus is alive. Many believe that there is a god, but you must make your mind up that there is one true God who gave his son Jesus Christ for you. Without this, you will not be able to understand the purpose of your pain and find the healing God wants to give you.

It is my prayer that you will get to know God and hear what he is saying to your heart.

CHAPTER 1
WHO IS THIS GOD?

If you can understand his being, then

you can understand his ways.

Who is this God? God introduced himself to Moses as he encountered the burning bush. In the Old Testament of the Bible we learn that Moses was an Israelite whose mother hid him in the Nile river to save his life as Pharaoh had ordered the death of all newborn Hebrew boys to reduce the Israelite population. Moses was rescued and adopted by Pharaoh's daughter. He was raised in the Egyptian royal family until he was forced to flee after defending an Israelite and killing his Egyptian abuser.

Forty years later, God speaks to Moses from the burning bush on the backside of the desert. Exodus chapter 3 tells us that Moses was out taking care of his father-in-law's flock, when the angel of God appeared to him in the flames of the bush. He was intrigued immediately because the bush was fully engulfed but still standing. Here God began to speak to Moses about his assignment. Moses was chosen to confront Pharaoh, who was the most powerful man in the world at that time, and lead God's people out of Egypt. God identified himself to Moses as "The God of your father. The God of Abraham, the God of Isaac, the God of Jacob." Moses believed God and was willing to meet Pharaoh but wanted to know who he should say sent him. He wanted to identify God. In one of the first meetings with Pharaoh (many would follow), Pharaoh asked Moses, "Who is this God?" Often when we are asked who God is, we tend to answer *what* God is to us. That is important, but you can only truly define his attributes when you can convey his identity. The Bible clearly tells us who he is. He is

Elohim, the creator of heaven and earth; *Elohim*, the creator of man and beast. He is the God of the elements. (See Genesis 1:1-2 Amplified Bible) He is the Father of Jesus Christ.

The first thing we want to know when we meet someone is his name. Then, without knowing more about him, we attempt to analyze his character based solely on his name. If his name is a strong biblical name such as David, we may assume the person is a noble warrior. An infamous name, such as Nixon, may remind us of the negative characteristics of that particular person. Names such as surnames are simply passed down through marriage while others may be withheld due to the circumstances of the relationship. For example, a single woman may choose to give her child her own last name because the father is not in the picture. Or she may give the absent father's name to the child to instill a sense of belonging and worth.

Leah, the wife of Jacob, named her children based on the state of her marriage. She named her first son Reuben, meaning behold a son, because she thought that having a son would make her husband love her. Leah continued to bare children in hopes that it would cause Jacob to love her. However, her fourth child marked a change not only in Leah's thinking but in her focus. She named him Judah, which means "praise" and said, "Now will I praise the LORD!" (Genesis 29:35)

Names are important. They give or reflect meaning and significance in a person's life. Likewise, God's names are markers of not just his character but also his actions. He is the peace of Gideon: Jehovah-Shalom (Judges 6:24). He is the provider of Abraham; Jehovah-Jireh (Genesis 22:14). He is the shepherd of David (Psalm 23:1). He is Ephraim's Lion of Judah (Hosea 5:14).

If you can understand his being, then you can understand his ways. His names give us insight into who he is and his unlimited power! As we experience different trials in our lives, we begin to better understand God. When we are in turmoil and our minds need rest, we call on Jehovah-Shalom. We get better acquainted with the Prince of Peace. Oftentimes, this will lead us to the Wonderful Counselor. (See Isaiah 9:6.)

We must understand that "In the beginning was the Word, and the Word was with God and the Word was God. The same was in the beginning with God. All things were made by him; and without him was not any thing made that was made" (John 1:1-3). In other words, God is the beginning of all things, heavenly and earthly. In him was life; and the life was the light of men. His life is our light. It is how our paths are illuminated in dark and evil times.

CREATOR

God shares his knowledge with us, but

He is the true creator.

We just read in John 1:1 how God is the beginning of all things. He is the creator of heaven and earth. The earth was empty and black. The Spirit of God hung in the air over the waters. Then God said, "Let there be light: and there was light. And God called the light Day, and the darkness he called Night" (Genesis 1:1,3). God began to shape the earth by dividing the dry land and the waters. At his word, the earth grew grass and herbs, and the trees yielded fruit. God made the sun, moon, and stars before creating the animals. Again he spoke, this time to the waters, to bring forth sea life and birds. He wasn't done quite yet. "And God made the beast of the earth after his kind, and cattle after their kind, and every thing that creepeth upon the earth after his kind: and God saw that *it was* good. And God said, Let us make man in our image, after our likeness: and let them have dominion over the fish of the sea, and over the fowl of the air, and over the cattle, and over all the earth, and over every creeping thing that creepeth upon the earth" (Genesis 1:25-26).

When God had completely prepared the earth for us, he created man. "So God created man in his *own* image, in the image of God created he him; male and female created he them. And God blessed them, and God said unto them, Be fruitful, and multiply, and replenish the earth, and subdue it: and have dominion over the fish of the sea, and over the fowl of the air, and over every living thing that moveth upon the earth" (Genesis 1:27-28).

God shaped this world that we look at every day. In his genius, the mountains do not scrape away the sky. The water kisses the earth lightly and is contained in its space. God created, according to *Science Daily*, approximately 8.7 million species on the earth. Consider the fascinating pyramids of Egypt, neck-breaking skyscrapers of Dubai, beautiful bridges of Paris, and even the familiar roads you travel daily. All were created by human hands, but had God not created the complexity of the brain, man could not undertake any feats. In fact, it was not until God breathed the breath of life into man that man was even alive or thinking. In his wisdom, God gave man the largest frontal lobe of any animal created. This allowed man to be higher functioning in self-control, thinking, and logical thought (see www.livescience.com).

God created a body that could contain all the organs in their place. According to the National Cancer Institute, the length of the colon is approximately five feet, but it fits neatly inside the abdominal cavity. An adult human brain would be the size of a pillowcase if you were to spread it out. God fashioned even the strength of the bones in the body. The strongest bone is the femur and it can support thirty times the weight of a person's body (see www.factretriever.com). On a simpler level, how do the small feet of a baby balance the body? How do teeth come in and fall out when they are supposed to? How is there room for the mouth to grow so the teeth will not exceed the orbital sockets. How does a child's body continue to grow even though his head stops at the appropriate developmental stage? All of these things are the handiwork and genius of God. Who is he? He *is* the creator. We must be very honest with ourselves and understand that we will never fully understand him or grasp him. On this side of heaven, he is just too great for our small minds.

RULER

Divine alignment is the order

according to our sovereign God, not

according to this world we live in.

When we accept God as the creator of *everything*, including us, we give him sovereign authority in our lives. We look to him for provision, hope, and sustenance. We look to him for inspiration in our work, for guidance in even the little decisions we have to make every day. We thank him for providing for us and keeping us through the difficulties of the day. When we accept God as creator of everything, we see him as our all in all. Often, we can find ourselves working outside of him, though unintentionally. We begin to put our trust in our careers, our impressive education, our sense of self, but when we do these things, we become misaligned. Though we profess that God is our everything, we start to live our daily lives relying upon what we perceive as our strengths, resources, and thought processes. We are operating outside of God's divine plan. When we live as the head of our lives, then we are attempting to make ourselves equal with God, or worse, greater than God. This thinking will lead to mishaps, disappointments, and, ultimately, failures.

Let's look at Sarah, the wife of the Israelite patriarch Abraham. God promised Abraham that his descendants would be as numerous as the stars. Sarah overheard the angel of God telling Abraham that she would conceive a child, and she laughed. When God initially promised Abraham a child, Sarah was well past the child-bearing age and could not grasp having a child. She sent her husband to her handmaid Hagar to conceive the promised child. She may not have realized it, but when she gave her husband Hagar, she essentially took over God's place. In her heart, Sarah dethroned God in a misguided effort to fulfill his word.

How ridiculous we can be when God has spoken, and we want to prove it. Or we want it to happen according to our timing. Hagar bore Ishmael to Abraham, and Sarah's pain was magnified. Hagar gave Sarah's husband what she could not. The new family dynamic brought scorn and resentment from the handmaid and strained the relationship between Sarah and Abraham. When Sarah, at the age of ninety, conceived Isaac, the true promise, Ishmael was still there as a reminder that Sarah had stepped outside of the will of God. When we attempt to manifest God's promises, we must be careful that we are working in the will of God and that we are giving God the credit. We tend to mistakenly attribute success to ourselves and failure to God. The glory belongs to him and he cannot fail.

Divine alignment is the proper order. We must live and operate as the ruled and the ruler. Our will must be aligned *under* God's. It is the hierarchy by which we were created, continue to exist, and should now live. We must take our designated place beneath our supreme ruler, God. Why should we be beneath him? Flatly, we are ill-equipped spiritually to stand beside him. There is no searching of his understanding nor comprehending his being. The order of our lives should be according to our sovereign God, not this world we live in. This world lives by the adage – do whatever makes you happy.

We cannot fathom his understanding or comprehend his being. Isaiah says, "Hast thou not known? hast thou not heard, *that* the everlasting God, the LORD, the Creator of the ends of the earth, fainteth not, neither is weary? *there is* no searching of his understanding" (Isaiah 40:28).

Jeremiah picked it up and wrote, "For I know the thoughts that I think toward you, saith the LORD, thoughts of peace, and not of evil, to give you an expected end" (Jeremiah 29:11).

He was, is, and is to come. God's power and presence are unlimited. He does not require timepieces, calendars, or mementos. He alone is time. He is both the schedule and he is the reminder. We only know what he allows us to know.

A college degree, for example, requires a prior understanding and education. To matriculate through the many required courses to obtain the degree, one must possess a fundamental grasp of the language. Whether one is preparing to be an elementary teacher or a chemist, one must know *how* to read. That may sound very simple but take a moment to reflect on all the things that cannot be done without the ability to read. The very book you are holding would be useless. To have chosen this book, you needed a working knowledge of the ABCs. Without that elementary level of learning, there wouldn't be any degree. After the creation of man in the image of God, Adam was given the task of naming the animals (see Genesis 2:19-20). The Bible does not give an account of Adam having to acquire language skills before completing his task. He simply spoke as God had spoken. The knowledge that God bestowed upon Adam has been passed down through time. We now use the building blocks of the alphabet to build communication and our world. Had God not allowed one to even comprehend the basic alphabet, this would all be unattainable and difficult to understand. In fact, the origin of the alphabet required God. It is a foolish and proud way of living when one lives as though any success was obtained without God. Without him we can do nothing.

Jesus speaks a parable of a rich man who had such abundance that he ran out of space. He decided to tear down his barns and build bigger ones. Afterwards, he declared he would pat himself on the back and take it easy for many years. God rewarded his arrogance with death, but not before he called him a fool (see Luke 12:16-21).

One of my favorite preachers, Reverend Dr. Harrell A. Alexander, has gone on to be with the Lord. He was a humble man who understood that without God he could do nothing. Reverend Alexander was a chaplain for the Denver Police Department for over fifty years. In the early '70s the governor at that time called him to assist in calming the prisoners at the Canyon City Jail. He was flown there in a helicopter. He pastored Bethesda Baptist Church in Commerce City, Colorado, for forty-three years. I never heard him complain about what he didn't have nor boast about what he accomplished. When he shared this parable with his congregation, Reverend Alexander aptly titled his message "A Barn Building Fool".

The rich man had wealth, but he did not operate in divine alignment. Humbly we must submit to our rightful position. Beneath God. It is quite a basic notion. How can we place ourselves above him? The psalmist writes, in Psalm 91, that God shall cover us with his wings if we will dwell in his presence. To be positionally over God, would be to *cover him*, rather than him covering us. If we were indeed capable, we would have no need to ask the question, Why? When I think about the responsibilities of God, why would I even want to be in his shoes? How would I solve the problems of the entire world when my own life's issues are overwhelming and at times feel relentless? Do we want to bear the weight of making decisions such as who lives and who dies?

"See now that I, *even I, am* he, and *there is* no god with me: I kill, and I make alive; I wound, and I heal: neither *is there any* that can deliver out of my hand" (Deuteronomy 32:39). In the wildly popular movie *Bruce Almighty*, Bruce, played by Jim Carrey, is dealt a few bad hands and gets pretty frustrated with God. Ever been there? Well God, played by Morgan Freeman, decides to let Bruce try out being God. While he starts off enjoying the power he has been given, soon he is overwhelmed by the cares of the world. Although God allows him to taste power, he does not give Bruce supernatural intellect. His mind and emotions are still limited. Bruce is bombarded with prayers from all over and must not only answer them, but also decide what to do for those begging for help. It isn't long before he makes a ton of mistakes and eventually wants to be free of God's responsibilities.

Pondering this control should sober us. It should make a believer grateful for who God is and what he does. Not just in our lives, but in the lives of those around us.

LAW-GIVER

Mishandling God's commandments

and people can change the course of

your relationship with him.

"And so it is written, The first man Adam was made a living soul; the last Adam *was made* a quickening spirit" (1 Corinthians 15:45).

Man was created by God for relationship *with* God.

Adam lived in heavenly surroundings in the Garden of Eden. God gave Adam two powerful resources: a commandment and a woman (in that order). Mishandling of this combination would change the course of man from God's original intent to live in provision and harmony. "And the LORD God commanded the man, saying, Of every tree of the garden thou mayest freely eat: but of the tree of the knowledge of good and evil, thou shalt not eat of it: for in the day that thou eatest thereof thou shalt surely die" (Genesis 2:16-17). Eve did not heed the warnings and ate from the forbidden tree anyway. Satan deceived her and convinced her to eat. "And when the woman saw that the tree was good for food, and that it was pleasant to the eyes, and a tree to be desired to make one wise, she took of the fruit thereof, and did eat, and gave also unto her husband with her; and he did eat" (Genesis 3:6). Adam was supposed to protect Eve. Just as God was Adam's covering, Adam was Eve's covering and he disobeyed God's direct warning too. Theologians have debated at length whose fault and responsibility was the fall. One question I find most simplistic and yet intriguing is: Why did God place a tree in the garden that could not only kill man, but could so drastically change the relationship of God and man? Second, is man aware that his earthly existence does not supersede his relationship with God?

So why would God place anything in the garden that had the potential to not only kill man but to so drastically change the relationship of God and man? If we refer back to divine alignment, the answer begins to come into focus. Man was created by God *for God*. The gentlemanly qualities of God were evident in the creation of man. He did not tell Adam what to name the animals. He allowed him to name them. "And out of the ground the LORD God formed every beast of the field, and every fowl of the air, and brought them unto Adam to see what he would call them; and whatsoever Adam called every living creature, that *was* the name thereof" (Genesis 2:19). God did not come behind him and change the names. It was the beginning of allowing man to exercise the free will that God had given him.

The tree was placed in the garden to serve a purpose greater than food. It provided man free will, along with its dire consequences. God's original intent was not to be far from his creation but to bring his creation closer to him through obedience.

The Bible does not record the conversation between Adam and Eve, but we know that when she encounters the serpent, she repeats the commandment that God gave. Here is the true beginning of submission and, later, the start of equal rights when she is punished, just as Adam was punished. It's important to note that Adam took minimal responsibility for his eating the fruit. He blamed both God and Eve. "And the man said, the woman whom thou gavest *to be* with me, she gave me of the tree and I did eat" (Genesis 3:12).

Whether you place the responsibility solely on Adam or on Eve, the results are undeniable; the partaking of the fruit expired the lifeline of man. Death was now on the table.

REDEEMER

Jesus on the cross is a breathing,

bleeding example of our value to God.

As a result of their sin, Adam and Eve suffered serious earthly consequences in addition to facing mortality. They were banished from the place of provision and ease. Everything that they needed was given to them in the garden. Adam experienced the ultimate quality time. God walked and talked with him often. He had complete and total access to the personality, genius, and love of God. Adam and Eve strayed from this place of peace and protection. Ultimately, the fall of man caused our separation.

Our estrangement was never the desire of God. The holiness of God would not allow him to dwell among the unclean. Rather than kill his people, God accepted a sacrifice on their behalf. In the Old Testament, the Israelites symbolically used animals for atonement, cleansing, and restoration. Cutting the throat of the sacrifice represented the severity and consequence of sin. These sacrifices were insufficient to return us to God and give us eternal life. God sent his son Jesus – a holy, unblemished, unspotted lamb – to repair the damage of sin and redirect our eternal path. Jesus did not appear at the word of God. He was not created. He *was* the word and already existed. "In the beginning was the Word, and the Word was with God, and the Word was God" (John 1:1). He was there at the beginning of man's existence and witnessed both the joy of God creating man and the pain of God when man disobeyed. It was now necessary that Jesus dwell on the earth in human form. God sent an angel to a virgin named Mary to birth our sacrifice for sin; Jesus. Choosing a virgin to carry his son reflects God's high regard for both humility and purity. She knew no man intimately but conceived through the Holy Ghost (see Luke 1:30-35). Jesus' journey to the cross was one of grief, betrayal, disappointment, and pain. There was purpose in his pain.

So why would God allow his son to suffer instead of bringing man back to him with ease? Herein lies the brilliance of God. He looks at the big picture while we only see the messy canvas. God allowed his only begotten son to endure the life of man. He gave us a savior who could relate to our hurts. To our storms. Look at the life he lived. His mother, a virgin, became pregnant without knowing a man. This is miraculous and definitely reason for rejoicing, but, to the carnal mind, this is suspicious and worthy of scorn and ridicule.

He was left behind by his parents. One could make a case that Mary and Joseph did not keep a protective enough eye on him as parents would having foreknowledge of his great value. We know from Luke 2:41-49 that Jesus was teaching and doing what his FATHER called of him. How do we reconcile all of this? He was exactly where WE needed him to be.

Jesus was sought after to be killed instead of revered. His love and obedience to God was a threat for the existing government. Jesus was betrayed by one that he supped with. Judas was his "friend" but in the end only used Jesus for what he could get. Have you ever been there?

The years that Jesus spent on earth as flesh are a direct testament of man's journey and God's reverence for both growth and time. Although God could send Jesus to the earth as a full-grown human being having known no challenges, he sent Jesus as an infant. He walked the earth as a man, experiencing the temptations and forces of evil in the world. He endured tumultuous storms naturally, physically, and spiritually. He was well acquainted with our fears and suffering. It is an amazing act of God's love for us to allow his son to be humiliated and ultimately killed, though he did no wrong. He was then, and is now, a breathing, bleeding example of our value to God. As Jesus journeyed to the cross, God continued in relationship with him. In response to God's plan for his life, Jesus depended on that relationship.

Relationship is a relative term. It can mean many things under many different circumstances, ranging from just knowing an individual to cultivating a connection to sealing a bond. Consider the barista at your favorite coffee bar. You may chat often, but you wouldn't ask him to babysit for you. You may go to lunch with a coworker, but you wouldn't lend her your credit card. You might have a distant cousin with whom you only share a last name. However, Jesus didn't come to be an acquaintance or our relative in name only. He came so that through him we might have a truly functioning and fulfilling intimacy with God.

> The thief cometh not, but for to steal, and to kill, and to destroy: I am come that they might have life, and that they might have *it* more abundantly (John 10:10).

To have life denotes a way of living that is different from the world – from the unbeliever. Consequently, our relationship is evident by the way we conduct ourselves. It is our Adam experience. We can talk to him directly as the writer of Hebrews encourages us to "come boldly unto the throne of grace, that we may obtain mercy, and find grace to help in time of need" (Hebrews 4:16). We can walk with him and know that "the LORD thy God will hold thy right hand, saying unto thee, Fear not; I will help thee" (Isaiah 41:13).

To endure Calvary, Jesus had to trust his Father, just as the disciples trusted Jesus when taking up their cross to follow him. The death, burial, and resurrection were the redemptive acts necessary to put our hands back into the hands of God.

CHAPTER 2
SHOW ME HIS LOVE

The lover of our soul is concerned

about every aspect of our existence.

Love is an intense feeling of deep affection. Agape love is the love that comes from God. In the Greek language, used in Jesus' era, there are three types of love: eros, phileo, and agape. God's love is not brotherly love (philia) or romantic love (eros). It is the deep sacrificial love. We see love portrayed in the most popular verse in scripture: "For God so loved the world, that he gave his only begotten Son, that whosoever believeth in him should not perish, but have everlasting life" (John 3:16).

While that is the ultimate demonstration of his love, we must remember that this love includes correction, forgiveness, provision, and protection. The lover of our soul is concerned about every aspect of our existence. He proved this both in the garden and after the garden by giving Adam food to sustain him, area to shelter him, correction to fix him, and forgiveness to keep him alive. The law given to Moses in the Old Testament was to provide an acceptable social standard to conduct our lives. When Jesus came to take away our sin, he fulfilled the law and added to it mercy, justice, and love. This was the introduction of grace, meaning that we now live in love and submission to Christ. Jesus was not cancelling the law but adding to it the correction and forgiveness that sustains our relationship with God. As we are now living under the grace that Jesus affords us, no longer under the law, we have the added benefits that came through the life, death, and resurrection of God's son.

Though we have no cognizant memory of the first time God showed us love, we do have all that came after. God loved us before we were born. "Before I formed thee in the belly I knew thee; and before thou camest forth out of the womb I sanctified thee, *and* I ordained thee a prophet unto the nations" (Jeremiah 1:5). God's love did not start when we accepted him as our savior. He loved us first.

"We love him, because he first loved us" (1 John 4:19). If that's not enough, God proved to be the lover of our soul and love us first when he gave his son for a world that did not love him back. "But God commended his love toward us, in that, while we were yet sinners, Christ died for us" (Romans 5:8). God's love for us wasn't contingent on our position to love him back. Merely because he created us, he loved us, self-sacrificially and unconditionally. That is agape love!

The way *we* love can be quite conditional. It requires the other party to do certain things, meet particular standards, *and*, most importantly, love us back. That is not God's love! It is important to note that although he loves us without reciprocation, we still have to surrender our lives to receive eternal life. His love did the hard part; it made eternal life available.

God's model of love teaches us the various aspects of how we should love. His love should be extended through us. Our love for others should be a mirror reflection of the love that he gives us. It cannot be better conveyed than through the scriptures themselves:

Beloved, let us love one another: for love is of God; and every one that loveth is born of God and knoweth God. He that loveth not knoweth not God; for God is love. In this was manifested the love of God toward us, because that God sent his only begotten Son into the world, that we might live through him. Herein is love, not that we loved God, but that he loved us, and sent his Son *to be* the propitiation for our sins.

Beloved, if God so loved us, we ought also to love one another. No man hath seen God at any time. If we love one another, God dwelleth in us, and his love is perfected in us. Hereby know we that we dwell in him, and he in us, because he hath given us of his Spirit. And we have seen and do testify that the Father sent his Son *to be* the Savior of the world... If a man say, I love God, and hateth his brother, he is a liar; for he that loveth not his brother whom he hath seen, how can he love God whom he hath not seen? (1 John 4:7-14,20)

Propitiation is defined as atonement or, more specifically, an atoning sacrifice. In our daily lives, we witness those who confess to love God but fail to love those around them. If we are indeed created in the image of God, our love is the reflection of him. Some may appear to us in what we consider a smudged image. We wrongly place the importance on our perception of them rather than on the fact they still belong to God. The least desirable among us are the representation of God. How can we be sure? Jesus himself speaks of a day when our treatment of the poor and powerless is either rewarded or punished.

Consider the words of Jesus when he describes the end of days and who will be rewarded:

> When the Son of man shall come in his glory, and all the holy angels with him, then shall he sit upon the throne of his glory: And before him shall be gathered all nations: and he shall separate them one from another, as a shepherd divideth *his* sheep from the goats: And he shall set the sheep on his right hand, but the goats on the left (Matthew 25:31-33).

Jesus is very clear that the separating will not be done by other sheep but by the shepherd himself. Only the shepherd is wise enough to judge.

> Then shall the King say unto them on his right hand, Come, ye blessed of my Father, inherit the kingdom prepared for you from the foundation of the world: For I was an hungred, and ye gave me meat: I was thirsty, and ye gave me drink: I was a stranger, and ye took me in: Naked, and ye clothed me: I was sick, and ye visited me: I was in prison, and ye came unto me. Then shall the righteous answer him, saying, Lord, when saw we thee an hungred, and fed *thee*? or thirsty, and gave thee drink? When saw we thee a stranger, and took thee in? or naked, and clothed *thee*? Or when saw we thee sick, or in prison, and came unto thee? And the King shall answer and say unto them, Verily I say unto you, Inasmuch as ye have done *it* unto one of the least of these my brethren, ye have done *it* unto me (Matthew 25:34-40).

The righteous were confused. They were not aware that all they had done for those in need was done as if it were received directly by Jesus.

For loving in deed, they were rewarded with eternal residence with God.

> Then shall he say also unto them on the left hand, Depart from me, ye cursed, into everlasting fire, prepared for the devil and his angels: For I was an hungred, and ye gave me no meat: I was thirsty, and ye gave me no drink. I was a stranger, and ye took me not in: naked, and ye clothed me not: sick, and in prison, and ye visited me not. Then shall they also answer him, saying, Lord, when saw we thee an hungred, or athirst, or a stranger, or naked, or sick, or in prison, and did not minister unto thee?
>
> Then shall he answer them, saying, Verily I say unto you, Inasmuch as ye did it not to one of the least of these, ye did *it* not to me. And these shall go away into everlasting punishment: but the righteous into life eternal (Matthew 25:41-46).

The King considered the unrighteous' failure to meet the needs of others as a personal slap in *his* face. They were cursed and sent to join the devil and his angels for all eternity.

John, the author, admonishes us to be careful with love that is only vertically connected but horizontally limited. This love may be strongly connected to God but does not extend to our neighbors. It readily reaches up but fails to reach out. We must love like God loves.

HIS LOVE FORGIVES

God can see you afar off, and he

anxiously awaits you!

The parable of the prodigal son is a good example of the love of God. The reason he is called the prodigal son is because prodigal means wastefully extravagant. He is the younger of two sons. He requests his father to give him his portion of the father's wealth. He receives his inheritance and leaves home to enjoy the spoils. He squanders it all through what Jesus termed "riotous living". I particularly like that phrase because it does not specify the act; thereby leaving the door open to insert our own misdeeds. It is timeless. A generation before me may have deemed that as drinking and partying, while the Millennials may see it as promiscuous living. It allows us all to fit into that category and relate to the young son. In addition to the way he lived, he took what his father had and what he would need later in life and wasted it all. (Taking from his father is in itself another lesson.) After losing everything, he joined another country and ended up working in a field feeding pigs. He was so hungry that the pigs' food was appetizing. The Bible says, "he came to himself". This is the moment that he realized that he had made a mistake. He realized that he should have stayed with his father. There, even the servants were well taken care of. He went back to his father expecting to be just another servant. He thought what he had done had changed his relationship with his father and he had lost his place in the family. He was wrong! When he returned, the Bible says that his father saw him afar off. That tells us he was anxiously awaiting his son's return. He ran to his baby boy and kissed him on the neck and then showered him with his best gifts. He put new sandals on his son's feet, the best robe on his back, and a ring on his finger. The ring signified a close and trusting relationship. He called for a celebration because he was so happy that his son had returned. There was no talk of his disdain, disappointment, or hurt behind his son leaving and losing everything. His son apologized for sinning against his father and heaven.

Meanwhile, the older brother was disturbed by the celebration and the lack of retribution. He felt as if he had done nothing wrong and yet was not given this royal treatment. Though this brother professed righteousness, it was in his profession that he erred. His attitude was not one of love but of judgment and arrogance. His father reminded him that he loved them the same and that he should be happy as well that his lost brother was found. This parable illustrates not just the love of God but the correct attitude toward our brethren. It is clear that we will make mistakes that will make others upset and pass judgment, but our focus should be on the love of the father. In his love he waits for us to return to him when we stray. His heart forgives and is made glad when we return.

HIS LOVE CORRECTS

The loving father corrects his child to

protect him.

As we have seen, our relationship with God hinges upon his love for us. As a loving father, he must at times correct us. "For whom the LORD loveth he correcteth; even as a father the son *in whom* he delighteth" (Proverbs 3:12).

We don't have to look far to see how correction and discipline is loving. We can look at our own relationships with our parents and our children. A child that is never corrected is spoiled and will have to live with being undisciplined for the rest of their life. That is not loving. On the other end, too harsh a correction is abuse and will take away a child's curiosity. Proper correction will give a child direction and help him to become a better person. Sometimes correction is the means to protection. When a child runs into the street we correct him to keep him safe. It is also a warning. Correcting him warns him and heightens his awareness that danger is present. Going forward, that correction may have to be given more than once, but the goal is to protect the child. The children of Israel found themselves in trouble many times when they failed to obey God. He had to chasten them in order to protect their inheritance with him, and their relationship.

Suffering was brought into the world through sin. God corrected Adam when he ate of the forbidden tree. Food was plentiful until God cursed the ground, causing Adam to have to labor and farm. This was to correct his behavior of disobedience. Moses had to be corrected also. Though he was a great servant of God, he made some mistakes that cost him dearly. He killed an Egyptian and later mishandled the God's people (see Numbers 20:8-12). The Israelites were sent into captivity for disobeying God and worshiping idols. God had warned them numerous times. Though each time they repented, it did not last long. Soon they were back to their old ways. When God allowed them to go into captivity, it was for their correction. God did not stop loving Adam, Moses, or the Israelites. Our mistakes do not remove us from his love. Sin separates us from God by causing spiritual death. But God has made a way that we can be in relationship with him, again through the death of his son Jesus Christ. Though we are his children, we fail, but we have assurance in his word that he still loves us.

But thou, O Lord, *art* a God full of compassion, and gracious, longsuffering, and plenteous in mercy and truth (Psalm 86:15).

We must never confuse God's love with acceptance of sin. He is holy and cannot accept sin. Even as his own son hung on the cross, God could not condone sin. God loves the sinner but hates the sin. When Jesus encountered sinners, he loved them and had compassion for them. He was greatly criticized for eating with sinners but did so as an ambassador of his father. He wanted to bring them into relationship with the Father. We must be careful that we are not indignant when entertaining unbelievers. It is the love of God that will draw them. Not our pious persona or preachy words. His love has to be the foundation upon which we reach out. Then we must allow that same love to send correction.

HIS LOVE PROVIDES

God's provision is tailor-made just for

your needs.

When I was little, my mother used to grow ivy plants all over the house. She was quite good at it. Her babies, as she called them, would grow so long that she would have to put nails into the walls to support the vines. Our living room looked like a tiny ivy jungle. Mama knew exactly what to do to make them thrive under any condition. I never doubted that she would do the same for me. She made sure that I had food to nourish my body, books to nourish my mind, and shelter to protect me. Just like her ivy, I was taken care of, but even more so. Instead of just buying me clothes, she took the time to sit and sew outfits just for me. I have to be honest and say that I did not appreciate being the only girl in elementary school with one-of-a-kind outfits. Of course, I wanted to wear the latest fashions. I did not know then that her designs were not for everyone else. They were tailor-made just for me. All the ivy plants looked just alike, but I was special. In those moments, she was teaching me about God's provision.

God is greater than my mother. Just as she loved and cared for me, God loves and cares for me that much more. He is our Jehovah-Jireh or provider. Jesus said:

> Consider the lilies of the field, how they grow; they toil not, neither do they spin: And yet I say unto you, That even Solomon in all his glory was not arrayed like one of these. Wherefore, if God so clothe the grass of the field, which to day is, and to morrow is cast into the oven, *shall he* not much more *clothe* you, O ye of little faith? Therefore take no thought, saying, What shall we eat? or, What shall we drink? or, Wherewithal shall we be clothed? (For after all these things do the Gentiles seek:) for your heavenly Father knoweth that

ye have need of all these things. But seek ye first the kingdom of God, and his righteousness; and all these things shall be added unto you (Matthew 6:28-33).

God's love for us is even more than his love for his own flowers. He makes sure that we have everything we need – and some things that we want. He dresses us in his finest clothes – peace, love, and righteousness. Mama worked two jobs at times just to make sure that I lacked nothing. God created the heaven and the earth so that we lack nothing.

HIS LOVE PROTECTS

The Good Shepherd can slay your

bear, lion, and Goliath!

My late Pastor, Superintendent Lamar Kennedy, was a man of great faith. He instilled the word of God into our church every time he mounted the pulpit. His profession of the gospel did not stop there. In the bank, he would tell you that God is good. In the restaurant, he would witness to the staff as well as patrons. One place in particular that he had a scripture at the ready was the hospital. When anyone went into the hospital, especially for surgery, he would pray for them. He was a towering man. As you lay on the bed looking up at him, he would offer a word of prayer and then he would grab your foot and say, "Don't forget the twenty-third psalm. The Lord is my shepherd." Why that psalm? Because it was about protection.

King David, the author of Psalm 23, grew up as a shepherd boy. He understood the primary role of the shepherd; protection and provision. David was experienced in caring for the flock and, as he penned this psalm, he likened the people of God unto a flock. He set the Lord apart in divine alignment as the shepherd. However, David makes this psalm personal as he too – even the King – was in need of protection and provision. Let's walk through the verses with David:

> The LORD is my shepherd; I shall not want.

The sheep did not have to provide for themselves. All they had to do was be sheep. They took no thought for where they would graze nor how they would survive.

> ²He maketh me to lie down in green pastures: he leadeth me beside the still waters.

The shepherd found the best pastures to nourish his flock. He did not take them to thorny or sparse places. His meadow choice was near the water they needed. It was calm and not rushing water that could sweep one of the sheep away.

> ³He restoreth my soul: he leadeth me in the paths of righteousness for his name's sake.

In this place, the sheep were not only nourished but guided, just as we are when we allow God to give us rest by following where he leads us.

> ⁴Yea, though I walk through the valley of the shadow of death, I will fear no evil: for thou *art* with me; thy rod and thy staff they comfort me (Psalm 23:1-4).

This portion has particular significance for David. While tending the flock for his father, David testifies, in 1 Samuel 17:34-37, that he slew both the lion and bear that came to eat of the sheep. When a lamb was carried away, David chased them down, rescued the lamb, and killed the attackers. It was this testimony that convinced Saul to allow David to fight the uncircumcised Philistine Goliath. David was victorious, as our God is victorious. The tools used by the shepherd were his rod that corrected the sheep, and his staff that redirected the sheep when they strayed. Our Shepherd uses his Word, His Son, and His Spirit. He even uses the rain. God can slay your bear, lion, and Goliath! Back to Psalm 23:

> ⁵Thou preparest a table before me in the presence of mine enemies: thou anointest my head with oil; my cup runneth over.

David was anointed King with oil. While it would not run down the faces of his brothers, it saturated David. That is why he said his cup runneth over. David understood that God could keep him in the valley, in the midst of trouble, and still satisfy his every need. A table prepared by God will have every good thing that you need. Not even your enemies can stop what God does for you.

> [6]Surely goodness and mercy shall follow me all the days of my life: and I will dwell in the house of the LORD for ever.

This was the closing affirmation and conclusion that God would never leave him nor forsake him.

Superintendent Kennedy was given the job of shepherd over our church. He took his guidance directly from THE Shepherd who had always provided and protected him. He knew that if he was good enough for David, he was good enough for us.

God is indeed the lover of our very soul. He loves us so deeply that he gave his only begotten son to be crucified for us. His love does not discriminate; it crosses all social, economic, and ethnic barriers, reaching us all. God is our loving father full of protection, correction, forgiveness, and provision.

CHAPTER 3
WHY ALL THE RAIN?

Where there is no rain, there is no

growth or vegetation.

Rain has many functions. Rain cleanses the earth; it provides nourishment by feeding the plants and making them healthy, and it gives moisture to dry places. Where there is no rain, there is no growth or vegetation.

Meteorologists forecast rain and monitor rainfall amounts to keep us informed of how much we get day to day and throughout the year. Too little rain can cause serious fire hazards. As I write this, Colorado has fifteen actively burning wildfires due to drought. Spring Creek, Colorado, has 107,967 acres currently burning, and so far, 132 homes have been reported destroyed and many more damaged.

Without adequate rainfall, our woods are in danger of burning away. California experiences fires that threaten homes and the livelihood of its residents. In the wildfires of Sonoma and Napa counties in 2017, fifteen hundred homes were destroyed, and twenty-two wineries were damaged. In contrast, too much rain can jeopardize our yards, homes, and cities as well. In August 2017, Hurricane Harvey ravaged Houston. According to the *Los Angeles Times*, Harvey was one of the costliest disasters in US history. Moody Analytics estimated the total damage to be between $81 and $108 billion. (Katrina reportedly cost $175 billion.) Hurricane Harvey set a record, according to the *Washington Post*, of dumping sixty inches of rain; the most from one storm in the United States. In addition to the sad casualties suffered, many families were displaced, and thousands of homes were lost. CNN reported that seventy percent of the homes affected were not covered by flood insurance. My own brother's home was underwater. We sat and watched the news as the rain began to fall. Quickly we went from being concerned to being afraid. It was devastating to watch people in rescue boats just trying to keep their families together and stay alive.

Rain in moderate amounts serves us well. It can bring life back to dried out land. Rain can cleanse an area of debris while nourishing the vegetation. Farmers look forward to spring showers because it prepares the soil for the maturation of healthy crops. If you have pollen allergies, rain is good. But if you are allergic to weeds, grass, and dust, rain causes them to break up and scatter into the air, which can cause an allergic nightmare.

The rains of Noah's day lasted for forty days and forty nights, or 960 hours of torrential torment. Comparing the rainfall of Hurricane Harvey and that of the flood of the Bible, it's easy to imagine the turmoil that the people faced. Hurricane Harvey only lasted a few days and it brought death and destruction. The people of Houston were constantly in danger. Can you imagine the chaos and the fear the people outside of the ark felt? I'm sure they were afraid for their lives and the lives of their children. I rarely hear anyone refer to the flood as a mass drowning, but that is what happened. Everyone drowned. The flood brought the earth back to a place of renewal and restoration. We, too, can experience new life after we have endured the storms of our lives.

FRESH START

Survival of the flood hinges on your

faith in God's assurance, and

obedience in building your ark.

During Noah's day, the world was very wicked. People were doing whatever they wanted with no regard for God nor his ways. It was time for a cleansing, a washing, a fresh start. Yet Noah had never seen rain. In the beginning, "And God said, Let there be a firmament in the midst of the waters, and let it divide the waters from the waters. And God made the firmament and divided the waters which *were* under the firmament from the waters which *were* above the firmament: and it was so" (Genesis 1:6-7).

Until that point there had only been misting to water the earth, but Noah believed water could destroy mankind and the world as he knew it. He also knew that God would protect him. He built the ark despite the scrutiny he encountered. He communicated with God and obeyed his instruction. Despite the obvious opposition, Noah *accepted* that rain was coming. There's a lesson here that is so plain we must not miss it: Noah didn't complain; he obeyed. How often when hardships come do you complain rather than try to understand what God is doing? It's strange how we expect to experience nothing but sunshine. Spiritually, we must *accept* that rain is inevitable in our lives. The difference between the believer and the unbeliever is not how much rain each will get but how each will respond to the rain. Noah's survival hinged on his faith in God's assurance and his obedience in following the specifications he was given for the ark in a spiritual desert.

The ark housed Noah's wife, three sons, their wives, two of every living thing, and seven pairs of every clean beast, male and female. The Lord shut the door and protected them from the flood.

So what was the purpose of this rain? God said it was for a **fresh start**. There are times in our lives when we have lost our way on the path God has chosen for us. We have somehow missed our turns and foregone our signals to halt. This results in us feeling overwhelmed, tired, and often frustrated. More important than our emotional situation is our eternal destination. God sent the forty-day rain to give his creation a fresh start, not just physically, but eternally. It was a reminder to the world how evil sin is, but in it was also a promise from God to never again curse the ground with floodwaters.

Maybe you are experiencing a flood of difficulties in your life. Could God be trying to show you something in your life? Maybe a sin to overcome or maybe as an opportunity to witness to someone else the proper response to trouble? Maybe to give you a fresh start and encourage you to build your ark? What is your ark? Your ark is where you find the most durability and the most protection. It could possibly be fasting or more prayer. It may simply be reprogramming your thought processes. Remember, we are called to "present your bodies a living sacrifice, holy, acceptable unto God, *which is* your reasonable service. And be not conformed to this world: but be ye transformed by the renewing of your mind, that ye may prove what *is* that good, and acceptable, and perfect, will of God" (Romans 12:1-2).

GET IN POSITION

Don't just get soaked – let the rain

move you.

Rain can also **reposition** us. It can remove us from a detrimental situation. We view the storm as destructive, but it can prove to be a beneficial catalyst for transition. Circumstances can force you out of a bad situation. For example, constant conflict on your job may be necessary to move you into a better position. Sometimes we will not leave a situation though it is painful and impeding our growth because it is what we know. We tend to be more afraid of the unknown than the situation we know, no matter how bad it is. Rain comes to remove us from our current positions.

Have you ever wondered why the people you started out with didn't last? Or why they slowly began to disappear? While you may have viewed it as abandonment leading to loneliness, it was really a flood that led you to God. It is possible that God allowed strife to enter to separate you from a stumbling block, to reposition you, and give you a fresh start with him. No doubt Noah gained a greater understanding of God after the flood, but what about during? It is in the midst of our trials that we are shown God's nature. In order for him to reposition us, we have to be attuned to him.

When I was little, it would rain heavily in Texas and sometimes it would even flood. I remember that even in the smallest of storms my mother would make all the children sit and be still. She would turn off all of the lights and make us be quiet. It may have been superstition or her respect for God, but it always calmed the house. Whether we are already in the flood or the waters are just building, we must learn to be still. Let the calmness take over us as God works. Noah's feeling of safety and peace came because of the rain. It was in the ark *during* the rain that he really witnessed the power of God to keep him safe. God locked the door and Noah had enough sense to not try to open it. In the movie *Twister*, a professor and her students chase a powerful storm in order to gather data with a machine. They left safe, dry land in search of chaos, turmoil, and destruction. At the age of 600, Noah trusted God and climbed into the ark. He endured and survived. Repositioning requires our focus to be on God so we can hear him clearly and follow his lead.

We see here that literal rain produced spiritual results. How is that possible? Nothing God does is one-dimensional. Don't just get soaked – let the rain move you.

GROWING PAINS MAKE US TALLER

If you are willing to give God your

reserve, he will send his word.

Sharndell Lowe is the owner of Cupcake and a Smile Bake Shoppe. She was a business analyst before opening her own bakery. She used her professional business experience to successfully transition from a home baker to owning a dessert truck and then to managing her own brick and mortar store in just five years. She co-authored a book about the lessons and strategies she learned along the way called *Entrepreneurship: My Story, Your Guide.*

After more than ten years of marriage – her first and her ex-husband's third – she got a divorce. She had one son prior to this marriage and her husband had two, so they were instantly a blended family. Sharndell admitted that although she was married for almost eleven years, there were signs of trouble all along the way. They needed healing from childhood tragedies, financial issues, and relationship difficulties overall. Sharndell often prayed from Isaiah 53:5 (But he was wounded for our transgressions, he was bruised for our iniquities: the chastisement of our peace was upon him; and with his stripes we are healed) over her marriage daily. She wanted God to restore her marriage. She was believing in God to move mountains and did not give up on his promises of Yes and Amen. Sharndell's marriage was never really a smooth surface or a straight place in her heart. She had insecurities and tried to hide the truth that her husband was unfaithful by switching the guilt onto herself. She realized after self-evaluation that she had unresolved unforgiveness in her heart.

Her marriage really began to crumble after she was laid off in March 2015. She decided that she wanted to pursue entrepreneurship one hundred percent. Her husband was not in agreement with that. He said, "I can't believe that you are giving up a six-figure income for cupcakes!!" That was the crushing moment when Sharndell realized that her husband did not support her dreams. At the same time, she knew her vision was God's vision for her life. She knew where God was taking her and that being laid off from her job had to happen in order to receive God's promises of Yes and Amen. Courageously, she went against the grain. She didn't fall back on her résumé. In fact, she didn't even look for a new job. Sharndell was now able to operate her dessert truck full-time and look for a physical location. God had given her all she needed to move forward. She found a building that was a second-generation space and opened her bakery in January of 2016. Though her entrepreneurial journey was blossoming, Sharndell's marriage was at a stand-still. She couldn't believe it. "How could the man that I had been married to for almost 10 years turn his back on me? After all, we also had a child together."

Before her professional success, in December 2015, Sharndell received a phone call from her husband's mistress. When she confronted him about it, he said he was sorry. She accepted his apology and decided to give him another chance. She tried to go forward, but the cheating never stopped.

Sharndell filed for divorce and removed herself and her children from the heartache and pain. "I cried so much. The hurt was so deep!! I had crazy thoughts go through my mind and hatred in my heart. But I had to pray and stay focused on what God had for me. You see with God; all things are possible. I had seen God move mountains and I knew that He would do it again. I had to execute my faith like crazy so that I could operate successfully as a single parent and a full-time business owner. God has never left my side. He has carried me through my pain. Now I'm walking in wealthy places and today is the best day of my life."

As a result of sticking to God and his plan in the face of rain, Sharndell has grown taller than her adversities. She has been able to reach her goals and look at life from a higher plateau.

In 1 Kings chapters 17 and 18, we see how the nation of Israel had turned from the laws of God and worshiped false gods. They no longer heeded the word of God. The Lord told Elijah to stop the rain. At Elijah's word, God gave him the power to stop rain from falling to the ground. It did not rain for three years. As a result, there was a famine in the land and the crops failed. This passage shows us the importance of rain to survive. Without the rain there is no growth or vegetation. Rain makes us grow; it feeds us. They needed the rain and therefore needed God, but he did not send his word to them. How can we appreciate sunshine without rain? Rain in our lives grows us in the areas where we are small. In this case of no rain, it was sin that caused the Lord to take the rain. Our disobedience hinders our growth in our relationship with God. When we are living in sin, we will find that growth has left us.

While there was no rain coming down in Israel, there was water available; a reserve, if you will. How do we know? When Elijah returned to Ahab a challenge took place. Both Elijah and Ahab's false prophets were required to dress a bullock, a young bull, and lay it upon their respective altars. Whichever God answered by fire would be the true God. The false prophets called out to Ahab's god Baal for hours, but he never answered. Then it was Elijah's turn. Elijah did not call immediately on the Lord. First, he requested four barrels of water to be poured over the sacrifice. Second, he called out to the living God to show the false prophets and those watching who was in charge. God sent a ball of fire down that not only consumed the bull but licked up the water too. Where did this water come from? It was a precious commodity and it was poured on God!

We may feel like we are in a drought and we have nothing left, but there is a reserve that keeps us going. It keeps us praying even when we can't find the words. The spirit makes intercession. If you are willing to trust God when it seems you have nothing left, he will take care of you. He will give you the opportunity to really grow – whether you are experiencing rain or famine. Sharndell's marriage was full of torrential rain and at the same time she was starving for the emotional care she was promised. God carried her through her lack and brought her to a place of plenty. The enemy challenged her mind, but God sent his peace to comfort her and his word to grow her.

Once again, we see how literal rain produces spiritual benefits.

GETTING IT ALL BACK

The rain will make your ground come

alive again.

After God burned up the Elijah's sacrifice, the people gathered the prophets of Baal and Elijah killed them all. He then prayed for rain and again God answered his prayer. In the case of Elijah, the rain also provided restoration. It restored the loss that the people had suffered both physically and spiritually. They welcomed the natural rain from God and no doubt witnessed the ground come alive again. Trees that had not borne fruit, flourished. Land that was once cracked and worn became green and moist. We may be experiencing a volume of rain that we feel is unbearable, but would we prefer the dry barren land of our soul? Would it be better to wither and die in sin or to be nourished by God in relationship?

Consider the life of Job. Job was a man who loved God. He rose daily to pray for himself, his wife, his seven sons and three daughters. Job was a wealthy man who owned thousands of cattle and had many servants. His social status is presented in the Bible as "the greatest of all the men of the east" (Job 1:3). Job had a strong relationship with God. Not only did *he* know God, but God knew *him* and his character. God testified to this character when Satan was looking for someone on the earth to test. The Lord asked if he had considered the upright and perfect Job? This spoke volumes. He was a true servant. Satan immediately pointed out that Job had a reason to serve God. It was surely because of all God had given him and how God continually protected all Job had. Satan challenged Job's loyalty and God's trust in Job by suggesting that God allow him to take it all away. He was sure that if Job lost everything, he would curse God to his face. God didn't waver in his testimony of Job. He granted Satan permission to touch all that belonged to Job but cautioned Satan not to hurt him.

Job's children were having a party at the oldest son's home when Job was informed that his oxen and donkeys had been stolen and the field hands killed. While this message was being delivered, another messenger came to let Job know that lightning had struck the sheep and the shepherds; they were all burned up. The next messenger came to tell Job that the camels had been raided, and the camel riders massacred. As if this wasn't enough, yet another messenger came to give Job the worst news yet: his children had all been killed in a tornado. It had struck the house they were in, causing it to collapse on the children.

Understandably, Job was distraught. Nevertheless, he ripped off his robe, shaved his head in grief, and worshiped God (see Job chapter 1). It is not recorded that he overheard the conversation between God and Satan. Even without being privy to that information, blindly, Job endured, and did not charge God foolishly. We know that we "walk by faith and not by sight" (2 Corinthians 5:7). After touching his wealth and children, Satan was not satisfied because he had been unable to turn Job against God. He then wanted permission to sicken Job. God agreed but still did not give Satan authority to kill him. Job's body was stricken with sores and boils. His own wife was so disgusted that she admonished Job to curse God and die. Job held his ground (see Job 2:10).

After losing his wealth, health, children, and support of his wife, Job faced another loss: his peers. His "friends" found it easy and acceptable to criticize Job as he went through all of this. Just as Job's friends blamed him for his trouble, we may find other people blaming us for tough times in our lives. Blaming us when we are in a storm. It was assumed and accused that Job's suffering was a direct result of sin. This mistake cost him the compassion of his peers (see Job 2:11,13). It even affected Job's relationship with God. The more they spoke, Job began to complain about his misery. He became physically and emotionally exhausted. He became bitter. After much discussion, the Lord had to step in and realign Job's thinking. God spoke to him out of the whirlwind (storm). Job was *in* a storm but could still hear God. Can we? Or is the storm too loud for us? Are we so focused on our problems that we no longer hear God? Job's response lets us know that he acknowledged the sovereignty of God, his own vile ways, and his submission to discipline. Like Job, we may find ourselves complaining about our misery. We may become exhausted and bitter. However, as children of the living God, we will be rebuked as Job was and should eventually lay our hands upon our mouths and proceed no further.

When we face our trials and tribulations, we should pause and consider the honor it is to be chosen *to suffer*. "For I reckon that the sufferings of this present time *are* not worthy *to be compared* with the glory which shall be revealed in us" (Romans 8:18). To be endorsed by God as a candidate to reflect God is a testament of his trust in us. It means he has looked around for someone who will give him glory in spite of their situation, and he decided on us. This is a healthy and rewarding perspective. You were handpicked to be his reflection on earth. Job was personally suggested to endure the hardship of loss. He was handpicked to lose wealth, health, and family. Have you ever asked yourself, why me? Job wondered too. Job is not presented to be flawless or even understanding. As you further read his story you see that this suffering took its toll on him. After all, he was human. God doesn't expect us to understand everything. How can we? We don't have all the facts. Nor does he expect us to never have questions. He does, however, expect us to seek him. "In all thy ways acknowledge him, and he shall direct thy paths" (Proverbs 3:6).

By chapter 42, Job is worshiping the Lord, and he is restored. All of his sisters, brothers, and friends come to celebrate with Job, bringing with them gifts of money and gold. Job's latter days are greater than his former: "for he had fourteen thousand sheep, and six thousand camels, and a thousand yoke of oxen, and a thousand she asses. He had also seven sons and three daughters."

What lessons are learned from God allowing this rain in Job's life?

God's trust will go as far as the relationship you develop with him. While you may not feel worthy of his trust, he knows the investment that he has in you and how you strive to please him. God will brag about your love for him, which in turn is God bragging about his love for you! He will consider and choose you because of your strength in him. God will never leave you to suffer but give you a deeper revelation of who he is. Your faith will grow as you suffer and impact the faith of those around you.

If Job had not gone through his trial, this account may not have made it to us. His suffering gives hope thousands of years after he was chosen. Not only will God bring you through, but he will restore everything you've lost in the process.

RENEWAL AND REFRESHING

A flashback of your tomb will catapult

your faith to the heavens.

The Jews in Bethany sought to stone Jesus and the disciples did not want to return there. Jesus was not afraid. When he returned, the relationship with Mary and Martha was changed through their interaction with him. They knew Jesus to be the resurrection at the last day but learned *that day* that he is life for us here on earth, if we only believe.

Though Jesus considered Lazarus to be his friend, he did not come when word came that Lazarus was sick unto death. Jesus allowed him to suffer, die, and be buried. When Jesus came, Mary and Martha, Lazarus' sisters, were grief stricken. They were so upset that Jesus had not stopped what he was doing and come right away. They knew that if he had, then Lazarus would be healed. Martha, the more outspoken of the two, flat-out confronted Jesus.

We should definitely take note of several things at work in this passage. It opens with identifying the relationship between this family and Jesus. He was not a stranger that they sent for in a time of need. When we find ourselves sin sick, physically sick, or even mentally impaired, our call should be for Jesus. They knew who could help them in this dire situation. They did not rely on the strengths or knowledge of each other. While the sisters' personalities were very different (see Luke 10:38-42), they agreed when it counted. They sent for Jesus.

They did not just say "Lazarus is sick," but they said, "whom thou lovest is sick" (John 11:3). Their reaching out made it clear that they expected Lazarus to possibly die. When Jesus heard, he immediately responded that Lazarus is not sick only to die, but to glorify God and his son. Jesus was in no hurry; he knew what they did not. Though they grieved, Jesus knew he would raise Lazarus for all to see.

When Jesus talked to the disciples, they were lost. They had no idea that Lazarus had died; they thought he was literally sleeping. We, too, read the word of God at times and do not quite comprehend what God is trying to tell us. This isn't meant to be a negative observation; it simply means when we have a carnal point of view, we can't perceive the spiritual.

Back to the rain. We can consider the awful rain that the sisters endured but let's not forget that while all of this is transpiring, poor Lazarus is dead. What can be worse? Have you ever felt like God has forgotten you? You love him and *know* he loves you, but where is he? Why doesn't he come right away? Why did Lazarus have to die? Can you imagine? Think about how long that felt for Lazarus. "But beloved, be not ignorant of this one thing, that one day *is* with the Lord as a thousand years, and a thousand years as one day" (2 Peter 3:8). I think Lazarus went down into the burial one way, but was raised, refreshed, and renewed in a way we cannot imagine. How he must have learned of God's true love for him! Can you imagine how this event catapulted his faith into the heavens? How much Jesus really did love him!

When Lazarus rose, he was still wearing grave clothes. No doubt they were stinking and sticky with rotting flesh. Sometimes we go through situations that cause us to lose our grip. Our faith gets sticky, our hope dries up, and then we feel as if God has left us to die in our situation. But then he shows up and gets us up. We can suddenly breathe again, and the grave clothes fall off as we jump around and praise him for renewing us, before we even know it we are having a Lazarus experience. Can you imagine the testimony that he brought throughout the land? No doubt there wasn't a seat that could hold his praise! Whenever he went through something, all he needed was a flashback of the tomb and he knew that God was real, and he was able.

This rain accomplished exactly what Jesus said it would. Many of the Jews witnessed this miracle and believed in Jesus. Martha and Mary suffered rain in the form of the loss of their brother, but all of the siblings experienced new life. Lazarus received both renewal and refreshing, naturally and spiritually.

CHAPTER 4
IF IT AIN'T ONE THING, IT'S ANOTHER

Lay hold of your hope. God cares.

Clarity is often a byproduct of rain. After the rain, the air is crisper and thinner, and our visibility improves. If you are going through the rain, or you're almost through the rain, examine your ways, your associates, and your life to see whether you have allowed them to cloud your vision. I'd like to introduce you here to a young woman who went through an "if it ain't one things, it's another" experience.

My friend Courtnee Fields recently turned thirty-four years old. She is a daughter, niece, cousin, friend, mentor, teacher, and whatever else anyone claims her as. She enjoys writing, speaking, and inspiring others. Courtnee is truly a lover of God and his people. She lives to try to show people that she is fully powerful, free-spirited, a bright light of the world, who loves to dance but, comically, is afraid of falling in public. To try to stick Courtnee in a box and smack any labels on her would be fruitless because she doesn't like boxes or labels. I asked Courtnee to share her journey through the rain that changed her life.

"I really don't remember where it all 'started' per se, but I slowly started doing things differently. I think it may have been my journey to better health. I started tweaking my physical habits and I believe once you mess with one area, you have to examine every other area to come into alignment. Doing better physically led to wanting to do better mentally and spiritually. Spiritually, I started seeing things I didn't like and didn't want to become. So I was going on this path of 'enlightenment' and losing weight and working a great paying job and accumulating all the markers of success and had finally gotten into a relationship, and asked God the most dangerous question I am so glad now that I asked. I told him I was finally getting it all and I was so grateful, but something still felt wrong and if any of it wasn't what I was supposed to have, please let me know. I lost the relationship, job, car, money, my grandmother, and apartment all in a span of about six months. Oh yeah, and I gained the weight I lost back too! So here I am in just utter rubble, really feeling like I was missing the entire point. And let me say, this wasn't yesterday or last month. The slow fall started at the end of 2015 and I'm just now in the place where it is all coming back together. It became very ugly and I'm just now at the point where I 'get it' enough to rebuild."

Courtnee realized she was gaining all of the "stuff" so that she would feel worthy. All that she did and received was to prove that worth to the world. It was only when she lost it all that she finally found out "hellloooo, I just am worthy!" None of that stuff defined Courtnee, and she made the decision to stop running herself into the ground to keep it all. There was no reason to trade her self-respect nor empty her accounts all for church titles. This spilled into her personal life and she had to make the same decision. For the sake of having a relationship, she had tolerated disrespect. It had to stop. She didn't want to spend her life running a marathon because she knew nothing would be enough.

"It was all very painful and ugly to see in myself the need to use things and people to serve as a way to boost myself in some way. It was very lonely to get by myself and examine my relationships to see if I was genuine in them and see how I was hurting people. It was heartbreaking to have people say some extremely unkind things to me and even more horrifying to realize I had said some of it to others. I felt some days like I had to be the crazy one. Everyone else is going along and being happy and I'm miserable. Surely it was me. I felt every emotion in the book and a few that weren't in any book that I couldn't even quite describe. It was all very necessary and helped transition me to a peace-filled place, but along the way I won't lie and say it was pleasant! It was indescribable."

Courtnee concluded with this: "I would also offer that rain is necessary for growth. When I lived in Colorado and would travel to Seattle, I was mesmerized at how lush and green and beautiful it was there compared to brown Colorado. Seattle gets a lot of rain! Its beauty is made in the rain. Oftentimes we don't realize that it takes a lot of rain to get a lot of growth and a lot of beauty. I don't believe God causes pain to come into our lives, but I do believe He uses it and turns it into good."

Courtnee experienced rain upon rain and, through it, God revealed to her that he valued her greatly. Losing everything allowed her to focus on the most intimate parts of herself. Every time she wanted to run from the painful storms, she forced herself to face it. She allowed herself to feel misunderstood, judged, different, abandoned, and even crazy. She knew there was no easy route to healing, but that embracing the rain would strengthen her relationship with God. Courtnee expressed her gratitude for this "if it ain't one thing, it's another" period of her life. "It wasn't pleasant, but through it all, I found my joy, and a completely new outlook on every aspect of my life. My spiritual life is easier and more peaceful than it ever has been before!"

Courtnee endured trial upon trial. When it rained, it definitely poured. Sometimes, it seems like everything that can go wrong DOES. It sometimes makes us feel as if the flood has washed away our hope. Every way we turn we are swallowing water trying to keep our head up. It could be any combination of things that close in on us. All at the same time. This place often really has no name. When someone asks casually how you're doing, you cannot even respond. Not only can you not choose a description for your day, but you can't even think of just one thing! You end up saying I'm okay when truthfully you are anything but okay. You are desperate for someone to just listen, and they may be there, but you cannot find the words. You feel like if you start to talk, you will just sound like a complainer. Ever said, "I laugh to keep from crying," and then get to the point where you cannot even laugh anymore? You just sit and shake your head. This is "if it ain't one thing, it's another".

I know that this place can feel hopeless. I have definitely been there. The walls seem to be crashing in. In addition to affliction in your body, suffering in your wallet, and chaos in your family, you also find yourself feeling hopeless and alone. You want to serve in your home, community, and church, but you're running on fumes because all hell has broken loose in your life. If you didn't know better, you would think that God had it in for you, or that you must have done something to get all this pain. You may have even just said that you don't care anymore. It's my pleasure to point out that you still care. How do I know? Because you've picked up this book. You are in search of laying hold of your hope.

Courtnee said it best: "Lean into the pain and don't run away. There is a transformational purpose in what you are going through, and if you would just wait it out until you understand the why, the area can be permanently healed instead of just putting a band-aid on it. It is all going to be okay and God is with you every step of the way. All the clichés are indeed correct, and God will be your best friend."

Another great example of "if it ain't one thing, it's another" is the Apostle Paul. His life and writings are too extensive to print in this tiny book; he cannot be fully covered in one chapter. However, we can explore briefly the many obstacles that he faced during life after his conversion. He was a scholar, a man of great power, and persecutor of those that followed Jesus. He was "a Jew, born in Tarsus, *a city* in Cilicia, yet brought up in this city at the feet of Gamaliel, *and* taught according to the perfect manner of the law of the fathers, and was zealous toward God" (Acts 22:3). Paul persecuted the early Christians "unto the death, binding and delivering into prisons both men and women" (Acts 22:4).

It seemed to Paul (Saul) that his life was going pretty well, and he was already doing the right thing by God. Paul was on a quest to bind and slaughter any disciples of Christ that he encountered. On his journey as he neared Damascus, he saw a light from heaven that engulfed him. Paul was so overcome that he fell to the ground. He heard a voice call him by name *Saul, Saul, why persecutes thou me?* (See Acts 22:7.) Though he could not see Jesus, he responded to him as Lord. He was then given instruction that would seal his experience, but when he arose, he was blind. Of course, Paul's life likely was not completely without trial, but the Bible does not record the "rain" until after his conversion. Although we may be living a life that we think is pleasing to God, there will come a Damascus experience that will set us on the true path. With that will surely come rain. Remember that Noah did not know what a flood was, but he accepted that rain *was coming.*

When I study the conversion of Paul, I'm drawn to the fact that he was blinded. Why did God blind him? Our vision guides us. It is the sense we use to take in and process our surroundings. It can affect what we hear, touch, taste, and smell. Sometimes our vision alters the true perspective of a situation. It is skewed, and God has to blind us with rain in order to clear our mind's eye. Paul's view of his credentials and deeds caused him to be indignant and self-righteous. Losing his sight would prove to be only the beginning of his rain.

After becoming a follower of God, Paul was beaten and stoned for proclaiming the gospel of Jesus. While the church at Corinth faced false prophets, Paul wrote in defense of his ministry. He had to let the church know that he suffered for the gospel because he was a true believer. Hardship would come, but it was necessary to keep the work of the kingdom moving toward eternal life. He was beaten to the maximum extent of the law five times. Three times he was beaten with rods, and once he was stoned. Three times he was shipwrecked. He wrote: "I have been in the deep; *in* journeyings often, *in* perils of waters, *in* perils of robbers, *in* perils by *mine own* countrymen, *in* perils by the heathen, *in* perils in the city, *in* perils in the wilderness, *in* perils in the sea, *in* perils among false brethren; in weariness and painfulness, in watchings often, in hunger and thirst, in fastings often, in cold and nakedness. Beside those things that are without, that which cometh upon me daily, the care of all the churches" (2 Corinthians 11:25-28).

Paul sums up the many trials that he faced while trying to offer relationship with God. The rain he suffered threatened his very existence, but God continued to make a way of escape for Paul. When we face trial after trial, we must hold on tight to God. We have to stay focused on him and what he may be doing. We should count it all as joy to suffer for his sake. He will bring us through!

LOSS OF LOVED ONES

Put your trust in God's strength, and

your hope in his love for both you and

your loved ones who have gone home.

My birth mother Billie Aitch died in 2005. We had only begun to really enjoy one another. After the death of my two-month-old twin brother, I was taken to live with a relative. I never lived with my birth mother again. We had scattered contact until I was twenty years old. Fifteen years later, she was gone. It was a very difficult loss as she was a huge part of my identity. Although I never lived with her, I needed her desperately to be in my life. She was the first loss that truly impacted me. We had developed a wonderful relationship and it was over. As I replayed gathering with my family around her bed, I realized that my children would one day have to say goodbye to me. After losing her, I wrote my first book. It was never intended to be a published book. I just knew that there were things I wanted my children to know, so I started writing.

I did not know my father growing up. At my mother's wake, I met his family for the first time. They invited me to attend a one-year anniversary memorial service for him the very next day. So, essentially, I buried my mother on Saturday, and then met and mourned my father on Sunday. If it ain't one thing, it's another – that's for sure.

In 2011 my beloved godmother Waltereen Diggins became ill. I met her when I began going to Unity Church of God in Christ. To me she was the epitome of God's love and holiness. I wasn't there long before she took me into her heart as her own. In her I found the mother–daughter relationship that I so desperately craved growing up. You would think that after losing my birth mother I would not deny the possibility of it happening again. I used to say that God loved me too much to ever take Mother Diggins. Turns out he loved her too much to leave her here! Saying goodbye to her destroyed me. She was the nurturing, affectionate mother that any child would want. Whenever I cried, she literally wiped my tears and kissed my face, all the while assuring me that God, not her, would make everything all right. She was saintly in the sense that she loved God fiercely and lived all she could to please him. At the same time, she was comical and practical. She never stopped pushing me to grow up in Christ. One day, she closed her eyes. Devastating. I remember crying so loud and so long that I actually lost my voice.

I was in my last semester of college pursuing my second bachelor's degree when my birth mother died during finals. I actually turned in my last paper the day before the funeral. When I walked across the stage to receive my degree, my godmother was there. She folded me in her arms and kissed my face.

Also, during this time, I was trying desperately to take care of my mama, Marie, who raised me. She was in a battle with mental illness, and her battle became my own. At the age of thirteen, I became her caregiver when she suffered a dislocated disc in her back. Her health progressively failed all the while her mind betrayed her. Our relationship was strained and riddled with disappointment. Through prayer and treatment, her last four years of life brought us both immense joy. She was finally living a life without emotional pain, without mental uncertainty, and WITH a motherly attachment to me. I'm deeply saddened to say that it took that so long to find the love we had for each other. I know now that it was always there. The very next year after losing my godmother, Mama passed away too. Three more of Mama's siblings followed.

Sadly, I have known a great deal of loss. Since 2013 I've lost my pastor of twenty-three years, Pastor Lamar Kennedy, as well as Mother Betty Bell, another woman who took on loving me like her own. Pastor Kennedy embraced me from my very first service at Unity Church of God in Christ until his last service in 2016. He was a man full of love, compassion, humility, and faith! As if his congregation were his own children, he endeavored to instill those traits in us. He was a strong supporter of my family and never failed to pray for us. Losing him knocked the wind out of me. It was so sudden and unexpected, but I don't think that part matters to me. It would have hurt even if I knew it was coming. When he came in on his last Sunday at church, he asked me to give a mini-message before he preached. It was his custom to spring these requests, so you had to always be ready. As I began to share the word of God, I looked over and he was praising God! The smile on his face let me know that he enjoyed the message, but the praise in his mouth let me know that he enjoyed God more! I had the honor of being the last live message he heard before returning home to be with God.

I attended church with Mother Bell for a good portion of my time at Unity. She was highly anointed to pray. I can remember once when I was rejoicing after leaving the altar, she took my hand as I passed her seat, and I went down to the floor. The power of God was sweeping through the building and I believe he let her hold the broom for just a minute. As I laid out in worship, I could hear her keeping watch over me and interceding on my behalf. In fact, she begged God to give me what I needed! She was the angel that guarded my encounter with God. This was not an isolated experience. I am sure that most people that knew her have the same testimony. She was fierce about the people of God and would not hesitate to cast the devil out! And when she hugged you, it felt like she pulled you right into her heart. When my godmother passed, Mother Bell took me in her arms and said, "I can't replace your Mommy, but I can be Grammie for you if you want me." Those words meant so much to me! And she meant every word! She made a special effort to love on me in my pain and rejoice with me in my victories. I really needed her. In 2015, she slipped out of here to see God face to face.

It's painfully staggering to me to think of all the people who are no longer on the scene, who I can no longer count on. What is going on? I cannot tell you how many times I was told "she's in a better place" or "God loved them best". I get it with my mind, but it is a feat to make my heart understand the good in loss. I asked myself, "Why would God do this over and over again? How am I supposed to recover from it when it seemed to all happen at once?" The loss of so many loved ones in a short period of time, or even the loss of just one special person can send you into a tailspin. Grief does not trickle, nor does it pour. It drowns. The Bible teaches us to not be dismayed and to understand that we all must take this journey. Nevertheless, our hearts falter to reconcile what our spirits believe with what our hearts feel.

According to Grief.com, there are five stages of grief: denial, anger, bargaining, depression, and acceptance. Each person makes it through the stages differently. While one may not spend much time in the anger stage, another may find it difficult to move to the next stage. What happens when you are in the depression stage after losing one loved one and then you lose another, and have to start from the beginning? I can tell you for myself that at one point it seemed that the stages overlapped, and I lived in a perpetual state of grief. More than rain. What can be learned here?

God's love is infinite and limitless. The depths to which he will go for us is beyond our hearts' comprehension. Healing does not always happen in the way that we want or expect. Sometimes, healing isn't the passing from life to death as we see it. But it is really the passing from death to life. God's ways are not our ways, and we cannot always expect him to move as we wish. However, we can always expect him *to move*. He is with us as we mourn the loss of our loved ones. He wept at the loss of his friend Lazarus (John 11:35). Some say that isn't possible since he knew that he would raise him up, so why would he cry? Because he was part man and part divinity. And, again, he had to feel this pain that we as humans also feel. Losing Lazarus gave Jesus exposure to this struggle from a human perspective.

Loss gives us a greater appreciation for life and those we share it with. It is not our intent to take each other for granted, but it happens as we live our daily lives. We get busy and we are sometimes complacent. When we are already feeling bogged down, rain comes. Sometimes it is in the form of death. This is not to cripple us, but to harden our resolve that God is in control. We inadvertently allow people to become our all in all, and before we know it, we cannot function without them. We don't know how to exist without the strength of our father, the love of our mother. Jesus does not begrudge us that closeness. He loves his father and understands that we love ours. However, divine alignment must come into play here. We must put people in their proper place and proper authority in our lives. This does not diminish our love or even our suffering when they are gone. Nevertheless, this is an opportunity to polish our relationship with God; to put our trust in his strength and our hope in his love for both us and our loved ones.

THIS BODY WON'T COOPERATE

There's victory after the healing, but

there's glory in the suffering. Find

that glory and magnify it!

Being sick takes a toll on you as well as your family. Sickness can debilitate you and hinder your daily responsibilities. It can also be costly financially. Back in the Bible days, if a woman had an issue with blood (excessive menstrual bleeding), she was considered "unclean" and could not be part of the community. If anyone touched her, they too would be considered unclean for a period of time (see Leviticus 15:19-10). Mark writes about a woman who was hemorrhaging for twelve years. She spent all she had on many doctors, but they were unable to stop her flow. In fact, her condition worsened. When she heard that Jesus was near, she made her way to him. She braved the crowd for an opportunity to be whole (see Mark 5:25-34). We can infer, based on the law and biblical customs, that she was an outcast.

If you have faced a challenge or setback in your health, you already know the obstacles that can plague you. There are instances when a person faces repeated illnesses as well as compiled illness. One illness opens the path to the next illness. Medications that can afford some relief for which they are prescribed can also disrupt the body and cause subsequent problems. Handling rain in external areas of our life can be difficult, but an internal attack strikes an area that we cannot touch. Upon hearing that Jesus was on the way, the sick woman gathered her strength and her faith and ventured out, determined to be healed. In spite of the risks taken by mingling with the clean, she set out to be healed. Her courage and resilience are evident in her actions. In the face of a new challenge, specifically touching and then talking to Jesus directly, she trembled but fell to his feet and told him the truth.

This account by Mark gives us a glimpse into suffering in the body but also faith in action.

This woman could have given up at year three or year seven, but she endured. She never stopped seeking help. She finally found the right physician. This body of rain teaches us longsuffering and perseverance. We must keep the faith even as we suffer. There is glory after the healing but there is also glory *in* the suffering. It is our job to find that glory and magnify it.

WHEN IS IT MY TURN?

If there is something you want, you

must DECIDE to fight for it!

A person without spiritual gifts or spiritual fruit is considered barren. The natural state of barrenness is discussed many times in the Bible. Infertility is painful and exhausting. While talking to the women I know who are waiting to be moms, one question always comes up: When is it my turn? We celebrate Mother's Day, baby showers, birth announcements, and christenings, and we should! However, some in our congregations, workplaces, and families are experiencing a rain that few understand, but many face: infertility.

Meet Davida Daniels.

My friend Davida, born and raised in Milwaukee, Wisconsin, had been a wife for ten years and a mother. Since childhood, she believed in God. In addition to her love and devotion to her church, Davida enjoyed planning outings, traveling, and spending time with family and friends.

Like many women, Davida always had a desire to have children. Though she had custody of a wonderful three-year-old boy, she still had a desire for a child of her own. As a teen, she was diagnosed with polycystic ovarian syndrome (PCOS). PCOS is a hormone disorder with one of the side effects being infertility. As a teen and young adult, she constantly dealt with severe bleeding and pain (another side effect) and went to numerous medical professionals, but the only solution she was given was to lose weight. Davida used to bleed for months at a time to the point where she had to be given blood transfusions. She missed multiple days of school and work. As she got older, things got worse, and Davida was considering a hysterectomy.

Before Davida married her wonderful husband, she informed him that she was not able to have children. Although he believed that they would, Davida lost hope. She shared her story with me.

"For nine years, it was constant disappointment each time I took a pregnancy test and it was negative. All of my coworkers and friends were having children except for me. I would watch the news and see women leave their newborn babies in abandoned houses and dumpsters and that would chip away at my already diminished faith. We had people pray and fast for us, but I felt like nothing was going to happen.

"Financially it was very draining for me. A lot of the tests that I had to take were not covered by insurance. I was spending all that I had, but I was not getting any help. I was more frustrated by the fertility options. I had discussed doing fertility treatments, but those couldn't guarantee that I would get pregnant. I had considered even getting a loan or fundraising for the fertility treatment but had decided against it. It just infuriated me that I had to pay thousands of dollars in order to have something that ordinary women have on a daily basis. Spiritually, my faith was on a rollercoaster. Some days it would be extremely high, believing that the Lord would bless me, while some days it would be the complete opposite and believing that God had forgotten about me. A lot of times I would be angry and frustrated with God, wanting to know why I was going through this, but I was scared to question him."

In 2016, Davida's husband was sent to Georgia to train for a new job. He was away for seven months when Davida and her son had planned to visit him in Atlanta over Columbus Day weekend. They met in Atlanta and found out the training facility where he was living had been flooded by a recent hurricane. He was ordered to drive back to Milwaukee. On the drive back, her husband had to stop to use the restroom. While walking to the restroom, a man of God saw him. The man started a conversation and asked if there was something that he could do for him. Her husband asked the stranger to pray for Davida. Together they believed for a child. That November, Davida's husband returned to Georgia to complete training. She was home feeling ill and decided to go to the doctor, who suggested an x-ray. Before the test could be done, Davida had to take a pregnancy test. When the doctor returned, he said, "Congratulations!" Davida shares the rest of this awesome story.

"I was confused by his statement. He had to plainly inform me that I was pregnant. This totally shocked me, and I was amazed that God came through on his promises. Lauryn Denay Helen Daniels was born on June 28, 2017. She is truly the child that the Lord promised. God did not forget about me. I want to tell anyone in this situation to hold on. Don't give up. If it is something that you want, you have to chase it, even when you don't see it."

Davida is proof that when you think things are falling apart, they may indeed be coming together. When you least expect it, God answers prayer. He will show himself strong in your faith.

Davida experienced a rain that lasted for nine years. It is no wonder that she grew tired and frustrated. Have you ever wanted something so desperately, but it just seemed out of reach? Have you ever watched everyone around you seem to rock their blessing, but your womb is still empty? Be encouraged and know that God cares about the rain you are experiencing, just as much as any other affliction, and it does have purpose. As with the woman with the issue of blood, this rain cultivates perseverance and sole dependence on God. He uses this time to prepare you for the answers of prayers. Faith and gratitude will overwhelm you every time you testify of God's goodness.

Davida had a difficult time putting her words on paper because just talking about the pain brought up all of the emotions that had hovered over her for nine years. She found herself experiencing them all over again but knowing that it ended with victory. She knew that this time when she speaks about infertility that the ending would be so different. The tears would begin hot because of the pain but run cool with the sight of Lauryn. "My soul, wait thou only upon God; for my expectation *is* from him. He only is my rock and my salvation: he is my defence; I shall not be moved" (Psalm 62:5-6).

MAN CREATED RAIN

Making mistakes isn't new, but it doesn't have to continue.

So far, we have examined biblical characters and people who experienced rain through no fault of their own. Truthfully, that is not always the case. We all have sinned and fall short of the glory of God (see Romans 3:23). And many times, the consequences of our sins bring rain, not just in our lives but in the lives of those around us. David can teach us quite a bit about this.

King David was a man after God's own heart (see Acts 13:22). As a shepherd boy he killed the mighty Philistine giant Goliath. He became king after Saul was killed in battle. David was a man of war and fought many battles, usually in the spring. One spring, however, he stayed home. One evening, while walking on his roof, "he saw a woman washing herself; and the woman *was* very beautiful to look upon. And

David sent and enquired after the woman. "And *one* said, *Is* not this Bath-sheba, the daughter of Eliam, the wife of Uriah the Hittite? And David sent messengers and took her; and she came in unto him, and he lay with her" (2 Samuel 11:2-4). Bathsheba conceived, and David's rain began; a perfect example of self-inflicted rain. David committed adultery with Bathsheba and produced a child. To hide his sin, he orchestrated the death of her husband Uriah. To add insult to injury, Uriah, unbeknownst to him, carried the letter that planned his own fate. David further attempted to cover his sin and feigned anger when the messenger notified him of Uriah's death.

Not only had David committed murder, but his child with Bathsheba would also pay the price for his actions. The Lord was so displeased with David that he sent the prophet Nathan to him. Nathan told David the story of a rich man who took a poor man's lamb for his own sake. The lamb was all that the poor man had. He raised and nourished it with his own children. He even laid the lamb upon his own bosom. When the rich man had a visitor, he took the poor man's lamb and killed it. David was so outraged by the rich man's arrogance and greed that he pronounced death upon him. To David's surprise, Nathan informed him that he was the rich man and had done a terrible thing (see 2 Samuel 12:2-7).

The prophet Nathan then gave David a message from the Lord. "Behold I will raise up evil against thee out of thine own house, and I will take thy wives before thine eyes, and give *them* unto thy neighbor, and he shall lie with thy wives in the sight of this sun. For thou didst *it* secretly: but I will do this thing before all Israel, and before the sun. Howbeit, because by this deed thou hast given great occasion to the enemies of the LORD to blaspheme, the child also *that is* born unto thee shall surely die" (2 Samuel 12:11-12, 14). David repented of his evil and his son was stricken. He eventually died. David's sin sent rain to his house. He had allowed his kingship to swell his head. He took his position for granted and used it to take what did not belong to him. His sin was great, but he was still able to come to God and beg for mercy:

> Have mercy upon me, O God, according to thy lovingkindness: according unto the multitude of thy tender mercies blot out my transgressions. Wash me thoroughly from mine iniquity, and cleanse

me from my sin. For I acknowledge my transgressions: and my sin *is* ever before me. Against thee, thee only, have I sinned, and done *this* evil in thy sight: that thou mightest be justified when thou speakest, *and* be clear when thou judgest. Behold, I was shapen in iniquity; and in sin did my mother conceive me. Behold, thou desirest truth in the inward parts: and in the hidden *part* thou shalt make me to know wisdom. Purge me with hyssop, and I shall be clean: wash me, and I shall be whiter than snow. Make me to hear joy and gladness; *that* the bones *which* thou hast broken may rejoice.

Hide thy face from my sins, and blot out all mine iniquities. Create in me a clean heart, O God; and renew a right spirit within me. Cast me not away from thy presence; and take not thy holy spirit from me. Restore unto me the joy of thy salvation; and uphold me *with thy free spirit. Then* will I teach transgressors thy ways; and sinners shall be converted unto thee. Deliver me from bloodguiltiness, O God, thou God of my salvation: *and* my tongue shall sing aloud of thy righteousness. O Lord, open thou my lips; and my mouth shall shew forth thy praise. For thou desirest not sacrifice; else would I give *it*: thou delightest not in burnt offering. The sacrifices of God *are* a broken spirit: a broken and a contrite heart, O God, thou wilt not despise (Psalm 51:1-17).

Examining this prayer, we see the process that David took to restore himself to God. David didn't dwell on his mistakes but set himself on a course of repentance. David admitted that he had sinned. He did not try to blame Uriah or Bathsheba for his actions. He owned them solely and took them before God. He stated that his sin was ever before him. David lived with Bathsheba and lost his son. This was not something he could think of without acknowledging his murder of Uriah.

We cannot get away from what we have done. We can only bring it before God for forgiveness. David went on to admit that he knew he was wrong. He knew that God desired truth from him, but he failed. David petitioned God to change his heart. He wanted to be cleaned again and for his spirit to be pleasing to God. He understood that mistakes were not new, but he did not have to continue to make them. David ends his prayer with sacrifice and praise. The rain he created was used to wash a new path before him. David learned humility and compassion through his rain. God's love shone through when he allowed David to see himself; to see his own failure and come back to relying on God and living in divine alignment. This rain was cleansing for David. Though we make mistakes, we can still come to God and repent.

CHAPTER 5
IT IS OKAY TO FEEL LIKE THIS, RIGHT?

Don't link your feelings to your faith.

Faith is not an emotion; it is a

decision to believe.

Many people believe that when they come to Christ, life will be easy. This myth about salvation sets the new believer up for a rude awakening. Accepting Christ as your savior does not mean that trials will be no more. It does not exempt us from the pain of our circumstances. It does not mean that our negative emotions will suddenly disappear just because we are now on God's side. (He's always been on ours.)

Emotions are a necessary component to help us process and deal with our situation. They are an instinctual reaction to life's situations. Good things make us happy and bad things make us sad or angry. Our emotions help us process life's events. Throughout the Bible, God validates our feelings.

Sometimes we mistakenly link our feelings to our faith. Faith is not an emotion; it is a decision to believe. Have you ever been told when you are crying that you need to strengthen your faith or that you need to get it together? When we find ourselves experiencing trial after trial, it is normal to feel sad. It is okay to feel hurt. These emotions can stem from rain and lead us to exhaustion. Here are some scriptures that let us know there is relief from overwhelming emotions.

And he said, My presence shall go *with thee* and I will give thee rest (Exodus 33:14).

I will both lay me down in peace, and sleep: for thou, LORD, only makest me dwell in safety (Psalm 4:8).

> Truly my soul waited upon God; from him *cometh* my salvation. He only *is* my rock and my salvation; *he* is my defence, I shall not be greatly moved (Psalm 62:1-2).
>
> He giveth power to the faint and to *them that have* no might he increaseth strength. Even the youths shall faint and be weary, and the young men shall utterly fall: but they that wait upon the LORD shall renew *their* strength; they shall mount up with wings as eagles; they shall run, and not be weary; *and* they shall walk and not faint (Isaiah 40:29-31).
>
> Come unto me, all *ye* that labour and are heavy laden, and I will give you rest. Take my yoke upon you, and learn of me; for I am meek and lowly in heart: and ye shall find rest unto your souls. For my yoke *is* easy, and my burden is light (Matthew 11:28-30).

The Bible does not say that God created robots or computers. We are not inanimate objects; we are created in the image of God. If we know that our ways can either please or displease him, then it stands to reason that he is a feeling God. In fact, the Bible is clear about his emotions toward us. "For God so loved the world that he gave his only begotten Son, that whosoever believeth in him should not perish, but have everlasting life" (John 3:16). The depth of God's love caused *him* to suffer rain. Yes, even God has rain. He had to plan his son's death to reconcile us. That points to his desire to have relationship with us. God loved Israel so much that their continual disobedience greatly displeased and disappointed him. "Yet the LORD testified against Israel, and against Judah, by all the prophets, *and by* all the seers, saying, Turn ye from your evil ways, and keep my commandments *and* my statutes, according to all the law which I commanded your fathers, and which I sent to you by my servants the prophets. Notwithstanding they would not hear, but hardened their necks" (2 Kings 17:13-14).

Another important emotion of God is righteous anger – meaning his anger was because sin was committed and had to be addressed. The children of Israel rejected warnings, not believing that he would judge them. Their disobedience brought the wrath of God not only upon them but also upon their sons and daughters. "Therefore the LORD was very angry with Israel, and removed them out of his sight: there was none left but the tribe of Judah only" (2 Kings 17:18). When Solomon forsook God by taking strange wives and worshiping their gods, God became angry. "And the LORD was angry with Solomon, because his heart was turned from the LORD God of Israel, which had appeared unto him twice" (1 Kings 11:9). God is not stoic. He feels deeply about our sin and how it separates us from him. His emotions of desire, distress, and anger were all because of the rain man caused God. Created in *his* image means that we have emotions also. However, we must be careful that our emotions do not lead us to sin. Paul warns us to be angry and sin not (see Ephesians 4:26).

Our emotions are instinctual and inevitable in the rain. God doesn't want us to hide them, but to bring them to him and let him take care of us.

DISAPPOINTMENT HURTS

We don't always have control over

what we feel, but we always have

God's help with how we respond.

The feelings of sadness or displeasure caused by unfulfilled hopes and expectations can create a cycle of disappointment. We are sometimes ashamed to admit it, but there are circumstances when even believers feel disappointment. We serve a great and powerful God who is able to do *anything*, so when he doesn't answer a prayer the way we expect or think we need, or when he allows us to enter into a new trial when the last one isn't over, we *can* feel disappointed.

Again, this is normal, and God has provided, in his Word, help for us to cope with and overcome disappointment:

> Be careful for nothing; but in every thing by prayer and supplication with thanksgiving let your requests be made known unto

God. And the peace of God, which passeth all understanding shall keep your hearts and minds through Christ Jesus (Philippians 4:6-7).

And we know that all things work together for good to them that love God, to them who are the called according to *his* purpose (Romans 8:28).

For I know the thoughts that I think toward you, saith the LORD, thoughts of peace, and not of evil, to give you an expected end (Jeremiah 29:11).

Hast thou not known? Hast thou not heard, *that* the everlasting God, the LORD, the Creator of the ends of the earth, fainteth not, neither is weary? *there is* no searching of his understanding (Isaiah 40:28).

Let not your heart be troubled: ye believe in God, believe also in me (John 14:1).

The rain that causes disappointment can help us get perspective. We don't always have control over what we feel, but we always have God's help with how we respond to how we feel. For example, John 14:1 begins with *let*. That means that we have a responsibility, an action we must take. We must allow the scriptures to work in our lives through purposeful action. So how do I keep my heart from being troubled? First, acknowledge when it *is* troubled. Second, take action. I meditate on the word of God that soothes my heart and strengthens my spirit.

I'M ANGRY ABOUT IT

We get angry. God understands.

This one is a scary one for most believers because we understand that while our God is one of love, we know he is also a God of wrath. Throughout the Bible, we see God's anger and punishment for sin. When he delivered the children of Israel from Egypt, God gave them commandments and the consequences for disobeying those commandments (see Deuteronomy chapter 28). After they made it to the land God promised, Israel disobeyed God. They lived in a cycle of sin: receive warning, repent, and then return to sin. As a consequence, God allowed them to be taken into captivity to Babylon (see 2 Kings chapters 24 and 25).

God's love for his people was not erased by their disobedience. He sent the prophet Jeremiah to speak words of comfort and hope to Israel. They would be in exile for seventy years, but they would not remain there. Most importantly, God wanted them to know that they were still his chosen people. "Then shall ye call upon me, and ye shall go and pray unto me, and I will hearken unto you. And ye shall seek me, and find *me*, when ye shall search for me with all your heart. And I will be found of you saith the LORD: and I will turn away your captivity, and I will gather you from all the nations, and from all the places whither I have driven you, saith the LORD; and I will bring you again into the place whence I caused you to be carried away captive" (Jeremiah 29:12-14).

Though Israel sinned against God, he still loved them. Because of that love, they were chastised. Hebrews 12:6, I think, puts it best: "For whom the Lord loveth he chasteneth, and scourgeth every son whom he receiveth." If God did not love us, he would not care about our sin. There would be no reason for justice or sending Jesus. After being given multiple opportunities to change, like Israel, sometimes we still resist him and make God angry.

With that in mind, we understand God's anger with us. What about our anger with God? Do we dare to get angry with him? When we look at the state of the world, the evil in rulers' minds, the desire for revenge, the hate in people's hearts, and the valleys in our lives, we get angry. Thankfully, God understands this. We must be careful not to disrespect God when rain comes and blame him for the evil in the world because it is man who chooses sin. When rain comes it is likely that God is doing something good with it.

The psalmist, David, expressed his anger with God, when he wrote, "How long wilt thou forget me, O LORD? For ever? How long wilt thou hide thy face from me? How long shall I take counsel in my soul, *having* sorrow in my heart daily? How long shall mine enemy be exalted over me? Consider *and* hear me, O LORD my God: lighten mine eyes, lest I sleep the sleep of death; Lest mine enemy say, I have prevailed against him; *and* those that trouble me rejoice when I am moved. But I have trusted in thy mercy; my heart shall rejoice in thy salvation. I will sing unto the LORD, because he hath dealt bountifully with me" (Psalm 13:1-6).

"I will say unto God my rock, Why hast thou forgotten me? Why go I mourning because of the oppression of my enemy? *As* with a sword in my bones, mine enemies reproach me; while they say daily unto me, Where *is* they God? Why art thou cast down, O my soul? And why art thou disquieted within me? hope thou in God: for I shall yet praise him, *who is* the health of my countenance, and my God" (Psalm 42:9-11).

David wrote these psalms and we see him decidedly praising God in the midst of his anger. Also, Job had a good perspective in rain when he said, "Naked came I out of my mother's womb, and naked shall I return thither: the LORD gave, and the LORD hath taken away; blessed be the name of the LORD" (Job 1:21).

Perspective, coupled with honesty, is the key to dealing with our emotions. We don't have to hide how we feel. In fact, we cannot hide anything from God. Feeling guilty and ashamed about our anger will only drive us away from God. When we are angry, whether with God or others, we tend to isolate ourselves from prayer, scripture, and even worship. That is one of the worst times to separate from God. We need his love, comfort, compassion, and forgiveness to take us from anger to peace. We must take the example of the scriptures and make praise our final reaction.

I GUESS I FAILED

Under the shadow of God's wings, we

have protection and cannot fail.

Defeat comes when all of the other emotions collide and take over. If it ain't one thing, it's another, and we can quickly feel like we aren't going to make it. Have you ever said to God, "If you don't help me, I don't know what I will do? If you can't fix this, then I'm done?" I have.

When I tried to get help for my mother that raised me, I went to doctor after doctor. Every time I thought someone would treat her, I was quickly disappointed. I was told that because I am not her biological child, I cannot seek treatment or hospitalization for her. When I finally made it through the initial consultations, my mother would convince them that it was all me; I was the one with the mental issues and they should lock me up. One of the worst slaps in the face occurred when I took her to see her primary physician. He was out so she was scheduled to see the doctor covering his patients. I sat in the waiting area watching television and feeling pretty accomplished because we had got in to see the doctor. It can be quite a process when you're on a fixed income and do not have private insurance. While I sat fixed on the morning talk show, I was summoned into the office.

When I walked into the examination room, there were two doctors waiting. My mother was completely quiet and looking away from everyone – especially me. I was informed that the police had been called and I was facing charges. I was so confused. I looked from doctor to doctor and then at my mother. She was absent. The younger doctor reprimanded me for my neglect and irresponsibleness. According to my mother, she had been sexually assaulted, and I was to blame. She told the doctors that a man had come into her home using a key I had given him. This was all completely false. With tears in my eyes, I begged her to tell the truth. She refused to even acknowledge my presence. As a final recourse, I asked the doctor if he had examined her. No. Then I asked if he had taken the time to read her chart. Not really. I was livid! As a paranoid schizophrenic, she was prone to far-fetched stories. This one almost landed me in jail. And it wasn't the first or last time!

In those times that I felt hopeless and exhausted, I could not seem to see my way out and stay focused on the light. We serve a powerful God and we cannot be defeated. Let me be clear here, we cannot be defeated in the sense that God cannot fail, but that doesn't mean we won't feel as if we *are* defeated. Sometimes we just need to remind ourselves to take courage. The old gospel hymn says, "The Lord will make a way somehow." We just have to hold on and feed our hearts the word of God:

Trust in the LORD with all thine heart; and lean not unto thine own understanding (Proverbs 3:5).

I can do all things through Christ which strengtheneth me (Philippians 4:13).

We *are* troubled on every side, yet not distressed; *we are* perplexed, but not in despair; Persecuted, but not forsaken; cast down, but not destroyed; always bearing about in the body the dying of the Lord Jesus, that the life also of Jesus might be made manifest in our body (2 Corinthians 4:8-10).

And I will restore to you the years that the locust hath eaten, the cankerworm, and the caterpillar, and the palmerworm, my great army which I sent among you (Joel 2:25).

Teaching them to observe all things whatsoever I have commanded you: and, lo, I am with you alway, *even* unto the end of the world. Amen (Matthew 28:20).

Feeling defeated is not the end of the world and cannot be your final conclusion on the matter. Whether the rain is constant and overwhelming, or sporadic and often, it cannot defeat God. Under the shadow of his wings, you have protection and cannot fail.

I GOT QUESTIONS

If we knew it all, why would we need

God?

My nephew Addison Aitch is a bit of a chameleon. He can fit into any crowd, build a rapport with any person, and still secretly feel socially awkward. He's a critical thinker so he asks a lot of questions.

At the time of writing, Addison is weeks away from graduating with a degree in journalism. It has been a long, hard, and tear-filled struggle to get here, but he's finally making it happen.

I asked Addison to share a personal time when he had a lot of questions. Here's what he shared: "A little backstory to the backstory: I am nothing without my laptop. I keep my contacts on there. I keep a very detailed schedule of what I'm supposed to be doing at a given moment and the allocated time I'm using. And I write a lot. And I mean A LOT. If people could see the sheer volume of files I have on my computer, a majority of which never actually see the light of day, they would wonder what else do I have time for."

He continues, "But for someone as dependent on laptops as I am, I have terrible luck with them. My first laptop was a hand-me-down from my dad. The power cord eventually snapped, but the laptop was so old that they had stopped making power cords for that model a few years prior. My next laptop was a MacBook (that I didn't even actually want when I first got it). It broke when my first roommate accidentally knocked it off my bed while we were playing a video game. My next laptop broke for the exact same reason, except I was the one who knocked it off the bed.

"I couldn't afford any of those laptops and I promised myself I would take care of the next one and guard it with my life. And I did, or so I thought. I had it for three-and-a-half years and it never left the condition I bought it in. Except for a few stickers, it looked good as new. I had hundreds of writing files, a few books I was in the process of writing and the podcast that I had recently started with my cousin on it.

"Only one semester away from graduation and it was gone! My car was parked in the church lot when someone smashed in a window and took my book bag, including the computer. I was devastated. More than three years of hard work disappeared just when I finally started to feel like I was making progress. I felt lost. I asked God why this was happening to me. What possible purpose could he have for disrupting my life when I was so close to accomplishing my goals? Hadn't I proven myself to him? Hadn't I suffered enough? What did I do to be here? What are you trying to teach me? When I thought nothing else could happen to me, I lost my grandfather, whom I loved dearly. He was my rock. In a way I had never been before, I was unspeakably *angry* at God and I had more questions. How is this fair? What am I supposed to do now?"

Addison went on to share his turning point. "When I was at my angriest, someone sent me a story about Robert Herzog, gauging my interest in an interview. Herzog is the owner of ZogSports, a business specializing in recreational sports leagues. Herzog is alive today because he missed his train on the morning of 9/11. When reading the story, I was struck by a particular quote: 'God has a plan for you. You were meant to be here.' The article ended with him finding peace."

Addison is, by nature, inquisitive. His thirst for answers often lands him in heated discussions and debates about everything, ranging from politics to man's responsibilities in medical research. When his computer was stolen so close to his exams and graduation, he had some questions. Losing his grandfather flooded Addison's heart with even more burning questions for God, and he did not hesitate to ask them.

Relationships are cultivated through expression and communication. We get to know each other through observation of actions and what we are told. There are, however, times when what we are told and what we see doesn't connect, and that is when we begin to have questions. We find ourselves puzzled at the actions of others and sometimes even God. And this is normal. Just because we are believers, it doesn't mean that we never have questions about our predicament.

When my birth mother died I sat with tears streaming down my face and I wondered, *what am I supposed to do now?* When my godmother was diagnosed with cancer, I had more questions. While Mama battled mental illness, I asked God why I had to be the one to take care of her? What about my childhood? What about my own peace? My own health? My own happiness? God, when will she be healed? Who will pay the bills while I take care of her? What kind of relationship will she have with my children? The questions kept coming.

Back to my nephew. Addison called one day looking for answers to his latest debate. I remember how disappointed he was to find that I did not have the answers either. It was even more devastating to tell him that God is not going to tell him everything he wants to know. If we knew it all, why would we need God? That is not to say that we won't have questions, but we will not always have answers. God will ask us to do some things that just will not make sense to us, but he knows what is best. Let's look at Abraham.

God called on Abraham to take his son Isaac into the land of Moriah and sacrifice him. Abraham dutifully rose up the next morning to carry out God's request. He saddled a donkey and took two young men with him and Isaac. They traveled three days before they reached the place God directed them. Abraham told the young men to wait at the bottom of the mountain while he took his son up to worship. Isaac carried the wood for the burnt offering and Abraham carried the fire and the knife.

As they traveled up the mountain, Isaac realized there was no lamb for the offering. When he asked his father, Abraham simply assured him that God would take care of that. When they reached the place God chose, Abraham built an altar, laid the wood on it, and bound his son. Although Abraham loved his son, and God knew it, he drew his knife to kill his son Isaac. Out of heaven, the angel of the Lord stopped Abraham. He was pleased with Abraham's devotion and provided a ram for the sacrifice.

And Abraham called the name of that place Jehovah-jireh: as it is said *to* this day, In the mount of the LORD it shall be seen. And the angel of the LORD called unto Abraham out of heaven the second time, And said, By myself have I sworn, saith the LORD, for because thou hast done this thing, and hast not withheld thy son, thine only *son*: That in blessing I will bless thee, and in multiplying I will multiply thy seed as the stars of the heaven, and as the sand which *is* upon the sea shore; and thy seed shall possess the gate of his enemies; And in thy seed shall all the nations of the earth be blessed; because thou hast obeyed my voice (Genesis 22:14-18).

What an incredible request of God. What a fierce rain this must have been for Abraham to be asked to sacrifice the son he was promised. The Bible did not record that Abraham had questions and for that I applaud him, but I have questions! Why would God promise something and then take it back? Worse, ask Abraham to KILL his son? Obviously, God had a plan all along, but Abraham was not told the plan. What must his journey have been like when he looked into the eyes of his child? Abraham, in faith, tells the young men that he and the young lad will go up to worship and return again. On the way to the sacrifice, Isaac begins to take inventory of what they need. He soon realizes that there is no burnt offering. *He* has questions! As stated before, God had a plan.

God knows our story from the beginning to the end because He is our creator. We live chapter to chapter; sometimes sentence to sentence. We must be careful that our questions do not get us stuck and keep us from turning the page. That is where our relationship with God must take over. We have to know him for ourselves and know what he has said concerning us. We can also refer to what he has already done to solidify our trust in what we need him to do.

For my thoughts *are* not your thoughts, neither *are* your ways my ways, saith the LORD. For *as* the heavens are higher than the earth, so are my ways higher than your ways, and my thoughts than your thoughts (Isaiah 55:8-9).

Wherefore seeing we also are compassed about with so great a cloud of witnesses, let us lay aside every weight, and the sin which doth so easily beset *us*, and let us run with patience the race that is set before us. Looking unto Jesus the author and the finisher of *our* faith, who for the joy that was set before him endured the cross, despising the shame, and is set down at the right hand of the throne of God (Hebrews 12:1-2).

While we look not at the things which are seen, but at the things which are not seen: for the things which are seen *are* temporal; but the things which are not seen *are* eternal (2 Corinthians 4:18).

Wisdom *is* the principal thing; *therefore* get wisdom: and with all thy getting get understanding (Proverbs 4:7).

I will instruct thee and teach thee in thy way which thou shalt go: I will guide thee with mine eye (Psalm 32:8).

Questions are natural and nothing to be ashamed of. You may not have all the answers, but you have THE SOLUTION to every problem. His name is Jesus! While talking to my eighteen-year-old daughter Hannah, she unloaded a ton of questions about God, predestination, salvation, and even death. For two hours we searched the scriptures and each one led us both to another question, so we searched some more. The initial conversation was sparked by her thanking God for not letting her decisions at fourteen impact her life at eighteen. When Hannah entered high school, she began dating. Just like with any teenage romance, she was growing and changing. Her expectations and reasoning continuously evolved. Years later, Hannah realized that her thought process was no longer the same and what she thought was best for her at fourteen is not what is best now. Our two-hour quest for knowledge led her to this final conclusion: "When I get to heaven, I got some questions for God!"

I let her know that I've seen some things and have come to understand the sovereignty of God. He doesn't have to tell me his business. How he will move or how he will work things out isn't my business. If he gave me all the answers I wanted, I would surely mess up my whole life. This took us to Adam and Eve. Of course, my independent, borderline-feminist daughter was livid with Adam! I was drawn to a component outside of his actions, outside of Eve. I began to examine the *motive* behind their choices. The serpent deceptively offered them knowledge that would make them equal with God. That was the turning point for them both. It wasn't when he saw the tree nor when he ate the fruit. It was that brief time in between when he realized he had questions and he did not know it all!

I allow myself to wonder and to even ask questions, but at this point my desire has somewhat changed. When I get to heaven, I won't be asking any questions. I'll just be grateful I made it! In the meantime, I must get into divine alignment with God. If you have questions, ask them. Search the scriptures in your quest for answers. You may find what you're looking for, but, if not, save those questions for heaven. While you wait, if you line up and trust God, one day you will grow to the place where you realize you need God more than you need answers.

CHAPTER 6
OKAY RAIN, LET'S TALK

The teacher can only groom a student

who wants to be groomed.

I'm not at all what you would call a swimmer. I can handle enough water to bathe and shower. Anything above that and I'm nervous. I was pushed into a deep pool when I was little and ever since water has been difficult. I can remember going under the first and second time and then being pulled up. Everyone was laughing because they could swim. It wasn't funny to me; it was frightening and immediately made me sick. Isn't it interesting that water can be like air to some people and concrete to others? Water can definitely weigh you down, even if you are a good swimmer. Have you ever been caught in the rain? At first, it's just a few drops here and there but eventually you're drenched. Your clothes begin to sag and droop. Your pants are sticking to you and your shirt is all stretched out because water is heavy.

God understands that we are all individuals. He made us that way. We do ourselves an injustice when we compare our circumstances to one another. When I heard everyone laughing at the pool, I felt like they were better than me. Truth is that the other kids weren't better because they could swim. They just had the proper skills to make it. God will develop your skills at the rate you can absorb, and those skills will be ready when you fall into the deep.

So many times our problems are magnified when we compare our lives to those around us. We rarely pause to examine those other lives very closely. We look at the surface and draw a conclusion that is often faulty. For example, we look at the clothes a person is wearing and assume that because they are stylish, they are put together emotionally.

Or because they wear perfect makeup that they are confident. The truth may surprise us to know that the one who dresses so great is sleeping out of his car. Or the woman with the flawless makeup is hiding physical abuse. Because we don't know the inner beings, we begin to either covet their lives or criticize our own. Or both. We hinder ourselves when we think we are the only ones enduring the rain. While our rain may be different, we all have rain.

When we are more concerned with the gifts or lives of others, we are rejecting who God has made us. We are telling God that he made a mistake in our creation. He failed us. Instead, we should be looking for the things that make us *us*. The things God put in us to endure rain and glorify him.

We are all capable of making it through the rain in our lives. *How* we respond will determine the rain's effect on us. You may be asking then, "Why haven't I seen a change here?" In fairness, the teacher can only groom a student that wants to be taught. The great part about letting God be your teacher is that he has understanding, compassion, and patience. He will support you as you journey. He is the all-seeing God, and nothing we are dealing with is unknown to him. Not our circumstances. Not our abilities. Not even our thoughts are unknown to him.

King David acknowledges the omniscient all-knowing power of God. God knows every thought and word uttered and we see this when David writes:

> O LORD, thou hast searched me, and known *me*. Thou knowest my downsitting and mine uprising, thou understandest my thought afar off. Thou compassest my path and my lying down, and art acquainted *with* all my ways. For *there is* not a word in my tongue, *but*, lo, O LORD, thou knowest it altogether. Thou hast beset me behind and before, and laid thine hand upon me. *Such* knowledge *is* too wonderful for me; it is high, I cannot *attain* unto it (Psalm 139:1-5).

David begins with acknowledging God's relationship with *him*. Before he knew God, God knew him. He knew when David woke up and when he laid down. Having spent every moment with him, God understood his thoughts that whole day, even before David knew them.

The omniscience of God blew David's mind. He knew immediately that he could never be equal to God.

> Whither shall I go from thy spirit? or whither shall I flee from thy presence? If I ascend up into heaven, thou *art* there: if I make my bed in hell, behold, thou *art there. If* I take the wings of the morning, *and* dwell in the uttermost parts of the sea; Even there shall thy hand lead me, and thy right hand shall hold me. If I say, Surely the darkness shall cover me; even the night shall be light about me. Yea, the darkness hideth not from thee; but the night shineth as the day: the darkness and the light *are* both alike to *thee* (Psalm 139:7-12).

Here, David begins to describe God as omnipresent. There was no place David could go that could exclude God. Even if he left God, it was clear that God would not leave him. He would still have his hand on David. Trying to hide from God was useless because God could see in the dark as if it were day.

> For thou hast possessed my reins: thou hast covered me in my mother's womb. I will praise thee; for I am fearfully *and* wonderfully made: marvellous *are* thy works; and *that* my soul knoweth right well. How precious also are thy thoughts unto me, O God! how great is the sum of them! *If* I should count them, they are more in number than the sand: when I awake, I am still with thee (Psalm 139:13-14;17-18).

David marvels in God the creator. He gives thanks to God for the intricate and detailed handiwork required to create man. He is even more grateful for the care that God gives him. David knows that he is valuable to God!

> Search me, O God, and know my heart: try me, and know my thoughts: And see if *there be any* wicked way in me, and lead me in the way everlasting (Psalm 139:23-24).

David concludes as he began: as an open book to God to be examined and directed. David wanted his ways to please God.

David recognizes that there is no place that he can go, and God will not only know it but also be there. David takes great joy in the thoughts of God toward him. Though we have ways that are not pleasing, and we sometimes fail, we should attempt to see ourselves through God's eyes. He sees us in the large picture; the finished product. How amazing though that he works on us in the small pages and can still see what we will be! Even when we cannot.

God understands that, like Job, we can be weighed down by our suffering. He already knows that the intensity, the length, the source of our rain, and the repetitiveness of it all can take its toll heavily and pull us down. David models for us a response to rain that recognizes God is with us at all times and it is his desire to support us through the journey.

DON'T RUSH TO JUDGMENT

Rain and dirt can open your eyes!

Abraham was seventy-five when God promised that he would be the father of many nations. And that he would be given a child. Sarah laughed, not believing that God could do such a thing through her, so she offered her handmaid Hagar to her husband in her stead. Sarah's rush to judgment changed her home. Forever. Sarah's focus was on her limitations, not God's limitless abilities. It's important to note that this was not the plan of God, but it was Sarah trying to do his job. Hagar bore Abraham a son, Ishmael. Thus began the rain that fell in Sarah's home, surroundings, and especially her marriage. Hagar began to treat Sarah with contempt because *she* had a son by Abraham. Sarah was in turmoil, but twenty-five years after the promise she conceived as God said, and bore Isaac, the promised son. Ishmael later mocked Isaac. All of the fault does not lie with Sarah though. In fairness, Abraham had a choice. In fact, he had more than a choice, he had a responsibility! The promise was given to him. He did not have to accept Hagar as a means of obtaining the promise.

Like Sarah, who didn't believe God's power and rushed to judge his methods for providing a son, Jesus' disciples also rushed to judge. The disciples and Jesus were walking down the road when they passed a blind man. "And his disciples asked him, saying, Master, who did sin, this man, or his parents, that he was born blind? Jesus answered, Neither hath this man sinned, nor his parents: but that the works of God should be made manifest in him. I must work the works of him that sent me, while it is day: the night cometh, when no man can work. As long as I am in the world, I am the light of the world" (John 9:2-5).

Notice, the disciples, as we are sometimes, were curious not only about the man's condition but *why* he was blind. As we often assess a person's situation and begin to speculate and look to find fault that resulted in their problem, the disciples rushed to judge whether the man's blindness was because of this man's sin or that of his parents. It's not surprising that they did not consider that God wanted to show himself strong to all parties involved. I don't think the disciples realized that Jesus was about to work a miracle. He announced that he had to be about his father's business, which was bringing light to man. After all, Jesus knew that this day would come, and he allowed the disciples to be there to witness the glory of God.

Is it possible that God has waited to heal you for this time in your life? When the right witnesses are in place and you are open to healing? As we continue with this miracle, we see that Jesus did not speak the word and the man's eyes were open, nor did he simply touch his eyes. Both were certainly within his power. Instead, Jesus spat on the ground, creating a salve of clay, then anointed the eyes of the blind man, and then sent him to the pool of Siloam. (The pool of Siloam was freshwater and therefore a popular spot.) He used the dirt, the common, even the undesirable to bring about healing. If the man had rushed to judge Jesus' methods, he may have forfeited his healing.

Unlike Sarah, the blind man didn't rush to judge. He did not question Jesus' methods or reasons; he was simply happy at the prospect of being chosen. He was ready for the opportunity to see what he had never been able to see. He did not recoil at the means by which he would potentially be delivered. He only cared about seeing. Vision *was* his freedom. It would do us well to avoid judging how God will move and instead relish the fact that we have been chosen to receive his hand upon our situation. Even his spittle is anointed and can open our eyes; can give *us* freedom.

If we look deeper, we will better understand why Jesus declared himself the light of the world. He was not only the light this man needed but the light that the witnesses needed. Even those that were not yet on the scene. Us. He brought light to the man both physically and spiritually. Having lived in darkness all of his life, the man was given a new world; a new perspective. While he once had to be led around, he could now follow Jesus with his own eyes. When God works a miracle for us, he brings us out of darkness. We are enabled to follow him with our own eyes; our own faith. The man once had to use his hands to see but he could now use them to glorify his God. To touch Jesus. Those who had known him his whole life could now testify that he had been healed. Changed. The people who knew you then, can now see that you are not that same person. Your change is so incredible that some would rather believe you are just a "look alike", as they did this man. It was difficult to believe God had done it, but it was indeed undeniable.

Our rain may be blinding but it is for the glory of God. Is that because he is selfish or arrogant? Of course not. It is because he is loving and wants to gather as many as possible back to his father. It is his love that allows us to experience rain. In the rain is our strength and we are drawn closer to him.

MAKE PEACE

When you are in trouble, take cover!

We must *decide* to make peace with where we are. It is a decision that must take hold down deep within. It is the enemy's delight to torment the children of God. He wants us to spend all our time wrestling with our situation. This keeps us from rest and can potentially steal our faith.

The Apostle Paul said, "For I have learned, in whatsoever state I am, *therewith* to be content. I know both how to be abased, and I know how to abound: every where and in all things I am instructed both to be full and to be hungry, both to abound and to suffer need. I can do all things through Christ which strengtheneth me" (Philippians 4:11-13). If we decide to be like Paul, we can conquer our fears and increase our peace.

We often use the last verse very independently, and it is applicable. However, reading it in the context of rain, gives us another viewpoint. Paul's resolve was stronger because he had already endured so much. He almost treated it as commonplace instead of something out of the ordinary. This mindset kept him free even when he was locked up. It was the result of his trust and faith in God. He knew that, come what may, he would be victorious. Paul was not advising us to make peace with *staying* in the storm, but with *being* in the storm. He was not demonstrating a lack of care but a lack of distress. It's important to note that this came about through much prayer and experience in the rain. It should be that we learn as Paul did that as we experience diverse trials our confidence in God will grow. This can be very difficult if our faith is misplaced. If we are looking to ourselves or the abilities of others to help us, then we will not see the ability to make peace with our situation. As James wrote, we are to "count it all joy when ye fall into divers temptations; knowing *this,* that the trying of your faith worketh patience. But let patience have *her* perfect work, that ye may be perfect and entire, wanting nothing" (James 1:2-4).

Joy? Now this sounds ridiculous. How can we count what we are going through as joy? We can count our rain as joy by seeing it as an opportunity for God to move. Our joy comes from *his* involvement in what we are dealing with. He makes deliverance possible. When we focus on what he is going to do and not on what we are going to do, then we can have joy!

> Therefore being justified by faith, we have peace with God through our Lord Jesus Christ: By whom also we have access by faith into his grace wherein we stand, and rejoice in hope of the glory of

God. And not only *so*, but we glory in tribulations also: knowing that tribulation worketh patience; and patience, experience; and experience, hope: and hope maketh not ashamed; because the love of God is shed abroad in our hearts by the Holy Ghost which is given unto us. For when we were yet without strength, in due time Christ died for the ungodly (Romans 5:1-6).

The natural response to rain is to take cover. Running into shelter. God is our hiding place (see Psalm 91). When we are hurting, we can take comfort under the wings of his protection. Have you ever seen someone just standing outside in the rain, doing nothing? Your first thought was probably, why are they just standing there? Your next thought to look for shelter for them. They could just run over there under the bus shelter. Or use the umbrella in their hand. There must be something they can do other than just stand there. When you are in trouble, don't just stand there and take it. Make peace.

PRAISE IS ALWAYS IN ORDER

Praise is voluntary, but it is not

optional!

Can you still praise God in spite of what you are experiencing? There will be many times that will test your praise. After my birth mother passed, I returned home to Denver. I was sitting in church and the people were exalting God. There was a sound of adoration and celebration all around me. I sat there and tears rolled down my face. I wondered, *how can they be dancing all around me and clapping their hands?* I wanted to jump up and yell at them, "Don't you know my mother is gone? What are we celebrating?" But all of a sudden, kind of without my permission, my hand went up in the air. Then I heard words of praise coming out of me! My flesh was crying and gripped with pain, but my soul praised the Lord. That was the day that I knew my relationship with God was the real thing. That was when I knew that I really believed he was worthy. No matter what!

While praise is voluntary, it is not optional. A voluntary praise may be contingent on your circumstances, emotions, or the results you get from a bargain with God. God, if you do this, then I will do that. God, if you get me out of this, then I will never do this again. God, if you do this, I will praise you. I'm not saying that I have never said any or all of those. We all *get* to a place that challenges our praise, but we must *grow* to the place where our praise is not optional. It cannot be bartered.

A non-optional praise considers neither situation, feelings, nor outcomes. Praise is a lifestyle as vital as breathing. It happens because it's what to do to live. We do not wake up and decide not to breathe because we didn't sleep well, or it was too hot in the room. We wake up and breathe because we expect to live. Praise is not concerned with the state of people, place, or things. Its sole concern is *thankfulness*.

Praise means to express warm approval of something. In the Old Testament, we also see praise as a garment to cover us. Isaiah prophesied about the ministry of Jesus, "to preach good tidings unto the meek; he hath sent me to bind up the brokenhearted, to proclaim liberty to the captives, and the opening of the prison to *them that are* bound; to proclaim the acceptable year of the LORD, and the day of vengeance of our God; to comfort all that mourn; to appoint unto them that mourn in Zion, to give unto them beauty for ashes, the oil of joy for mourning, the garment of praise for the spirit of heaviness; that they might be called trees of righteousness, the planting of the LORD, that he might be glorified" (Isaiah 61:1-3).

The garment of praise is an opportunity to take off what we are going through and clothe ourselves in the Lord Jesus. He not only came, but he demonstrated his praise on the journey to his own death. He glorified his father and praised him even though he was being riddled with hate, betrayal, scorn, and lies. It sounds odd to an unbeliever, but the believer knows that praise is a weapon that will defeat the enemy.

In 2nd Chronicles, we see Jehoshaphat facing a battle. A large army comprised of the Moabites, Ammonites, and some the people of Meunim, are prepared to fight him. He was afraid and began to pray. He put the whole city on a fast to inquire of God. He took this time to remind God that he was the same God that delivered Israel, and that these people were trying to take away the land God gave his people. God sent word through Jahaziel, the son of Zachariah, that the battle was not theirs, but the Lord's, and he would give them the victory. Jehoshaphat prepared the next day and told the people to believe the word sent and bless God for he would go with them. "And when he had consulted with the people, he appointed singers unto the LORD, and that should praise the beauty of holiness, as they went out before the army, and to say, Praise the LORD, for his mercy *endureth* for ever" (2 Chronicles 20:21). As they praised, God set an ambush for their enemies and they were defeated. All of this happened before Jehoshaphat and Judah got to the site. The enemy were all dead and their spoil was given to Jehoshaphat. They never had to lift a finger to fight, just their hands to praise.

We must train ourselves to stop looking for a feeling to confirm who we are. We are praisers too. I don't feel brown. I *am* brown. No circumstance I face can change that. And nothing can change the fact that I'm called to "make a joyful noise unto God, all ye lands: sing forth the honour of his name: and make his praise glorious" (Psalm 66:1-2).

"I will bless the LORD at all times: and his praise *shall* continually *be* in my mouth. My soul shall make her boast in the LORD: the humble shall hear *thereof,* and be glad. O magnify the LORD with me, and let us exalt his name together" (Psalm 34:1-3). This scripture lets us know that it's not just a select few but all of us who are required to praise the Lord.

This place of praise is a place of maturity and lifestyle. Tantrums cannot last in this place. In this place you say thank you despite being in the rain amidst a storm. You thank God that things are as well as they are. I used to wonder why the church mothers would say that. Now I know that as bad as things may be, it could be worse. As you begin to breathe and live praise, be on the lookout for that "beauty for ashes" exchange the Lord promised in Isaiah 61. God has what you need. He exchanges his promises for our pain. He gives us his health for our hurt. Amazingly, he can make the ugliest situation beautiful in our sight, if we would only yield our praise.

If you cannot find the blessing in where you are now, you have two options:

First, look back. Take a stroll down memory lane and *remember* what God has done for you. Allow your soul to peruse the aisles of ashes you passed, the columns of confusion you conquered, and the ways you walked through when no way was there.

> For the enemy hath persecuted my soul; he hath smitten my life down to the ground; he hath made me to dwell in darkness, as those that have been long dead. Therefore is my spirit overwhelmed within me; my heart within me is desolate. I remember the days of old; I meditate on all thy works; I muse on the work of thy hands (Psalm 143:3-5).

Second, let your soul remember how it *felt* to come out of the rain the last time.

> Only take heed to thyself, and keep thy soul diligently, lest thou forget the things which thine eyes have seen, and lest they depart from thy heart all the days of thy life; but teach them thy sons, and thy sons' sons (Deuteronomy 4:9).

You will see that God did something for you that you could not do for yourself. The mind has the ability to time travel, to take us on past journeys that will propel us into our future. Use *that* praise to jump start *this* praise! Trust God to do it again.

Praise is not our approval of God. When we praise we are not telling God that he has finally got it right, but that he *is* right in all that he does. Praise again puts us in divine alignment with him because we humble ourselves and bow to his will. We praise him because we realize that whatever way he decided to move, it would result in the best move for us. It would give us the best outcome.

For a lesson in praising God in the rain, consider Paul and Silas. They were imprisoned for preaching the gospel in the face of a sorcerer. There are those whom no one expects to believe the truth when they hear it. A young girl met them on their way to prayer. She followed them and mocked them, pretending to believe. When Paul recognized the mocking spirit at work, he cast it out and she was delivered. Her deliverance dried up the money her masters gained from using her for divination. This angered them and landed Paul and Silas into prison. The guard didn't just put them in any cell, he threw them into the inner prison and "made their feet fast in the stocks. And at midnight Paul and Silas prayed, and sang praises unto God: and the prisoners heard them. And suddenly there was a great earthquake, so that the foundations of the prison were shaken: and immediately all the doors were opened, and every one's bands were loosed. And the keeper of the prison awaking out of his sleep, and seeing the prison doors open, he drew out his sword, and would have killed himself, supposing that the prisoners had been fled. But Paul cried with a loud voice, saying, Do thyself no harm; for we are all here. Then he called for a light, and sprang in, and came trembling, and fell down before Paul and Silas, and brought them out, and said, Sirs, what must I do to be saved?" (Acts 16:24-30).

Paul and Silas could have responded with anger or pity after preaching the Good News and being beaten and then thrown in prison. Under those circumstances, who would blame them? When we follow Christ, we will be hated, and thrown away by man. Remember, James exhorts us to, "count it all joy when ye fall into divers temptations; knowing *this*, that the trying of your faith worketh patience" (James 1:2-3). This was the case for the dynamic gospel duo. They counted it all joy, and it's evident by their response to incarceration. They did not take their frustrations out on those around them. They simply devised a plan. It was not to escape, but to give God glory. They did not use their praise to impress or oppress, but to lift up the name of Jesus. Their praise and prayer moved God. They were loosed without anyone's keys and yet remained in the prison. Praise prepared their hearts for deliverance. Ultimately, the guard was saved. God used the beating and imprisonment of Paul and Silas to send his word. The guard was so moved that he took them to his house, cared for their wounds, fed them, and then rejoiced with them.

There are so many lessons in this scripture: Learning to praise God in spite of feeling locked up and bound by our circumstances; giving ourselves to praise and prayer no matter who is around us; and not compromising the assignment we've been given to gain comfort.

GOD WANTS A WORD WITH YOU

Be transparent when you pray.

Vulnerability is an asset and not a

liability.

We have been given a lifeline directly to God through prayer. It is the moment we can be our most transparent before him. Our vulnerability is an asset and not a liability. Come rain or shine, prayer is always in order. Let's review the model of prayer Jesus gave the disciples in Matthew 6:5-13:

> [5]And when thou prayest, thou shalt not be as the hypocrites *are*: for they love to pray standing in the synagogues and in the corners of the streets, that they may be seen of men. Verily I say unto you, They have their reward.

Prayer is intimate and personal. Though it can be done corporately with a group, the sentiments are still very personal. God does not require poets or theologians to reach him. He only wants to hear our hearts.

> [6]But thou, when thou prayest, enter into thy closet, and when thou hast shut thy door, pray to thy Father which is in secret; and thy Father which seeth in secret shall reward thee openly.
> [7]But when ye pray, use not vain repetitions, as the heathen *do*: for they think that they shall be heard for their much speaking.

[8]Be not ye therefore like unto them: for your Father knoweth what things ye have need of, before ye ask him. Our motives are not hidden from God nor our needs.

[9]After this manner therefore pray ye: Our Father which art in heaven, Hallowed be thy name.

[10]Thy kingdom come. Thy will be done in earth, as *it is* in heaven.

Before we began to ask for anything, Jesus shows us the importance of divine alignment and reverencing our holy God. His name is holy. And his will is holy.

[11]Give us this day our daily bread.

Here we are advised to rely on him daily. Ask what we need without care for greed or stockpiling. Our daily bread assures us that daily he will provide and be with us. He will not pass out rations nor forsake us.

[12]And forgive us our debts, as we forgive our debtors.

This is usually a part that slows us down. Wanting God's forgiveness is obvious and natural, but receiving it being contingent upon forgiving others, *that* is the speed bump. It is sometimes the hindrance to our prayers because we have not forgiven. This is usually because of our perception or misguided definitions of forgiveness. We think it is a release form. A get out of jail free card. It *is* indeed both of those, but not for the offender but the offended. It is our ticket to peace and freedom. We may think the peace means we will never have to deal with that offense or offender again, but the true peace is that we will be in right standing with God and that our prayers will not be hindered by us.

[13]And lead us not into temptation, but deliver us from evil: For thine is the kingdom, and the power, and the glory, for ever. Amen.

Our hope is in him as we willingly obey and follow him.

We are wise to use this model in our prayers. Think of the word ACTS:

- Acknowledge
- Confess

- Thanks
- Supplication

Every day we should approach the throne in like manner:

First in our prayers, we should acknowledge the Lord is God. Of course, he knows who he is. The affirmation is *for us* to solidify his sovereignty within ourselves.

Second, we should confess our sins and seek forgiveness. We sin by commission and omission. Disobeying the rules and neglecting directives. It is important to recognize both. As we are clearing our path with God, we must not forget to extend forgiveness as well.

Third, we should be thankful for his provision. Even as we go through rain, he continues to sustain us.

Finally, we should bring our supplications to the Lord and ask him for help in all areas of life, from paying bills to understanding why we are going through the rain.

We have access to the Father at all times. We can come boldly before the throne (Hebrews 4:16). There is no clock that times us nor guards we must pass. If we ever feel like we should be able to handle things on our own, we deceive ourselves. Even Jesus prayed. He was always leaving his disciples to pray. After he "sent the multitudes away, he went up into a mountain apart to pray: and when the evening was come, he was there alone" (Matthew 14:23). And then in the Garden of Gethsemane, just before he was crucified, he said "unto the disciples, Sit ye here, while I go and pray yonder" (Matthew 26:36).

Jesus takes the time to pray for us. He told Simon, "And the Lord said, Simon, Simon, behold, Satan hath desired *to have* you, that ye may sift *you* as wheat: but I have prayed for thee, that thy faith fail not: and when thou art converted, strengthen thy brethren" (Luke 22:31-32). In Romans 8:34, Paul says that Christ "who is even at the right hand of God, who also maketh intercession for us".

Who could be a better prayer partner? Who has more faith? Who has endured more rain than Jesus? And, best of all, who knows the Father better than his only begotten son?

Gods wants to hear our desires. We see the intimacy of prayer when Hannah sought God for a child. Yearly, Elkanah took his family out of the city to worship in Shiloh. Hannah's worship time was often disturbed by the mocking of Peninnah, Elkanah's other wife. Peninnah thought it was her duty to taunt Hannah because she was barren. Hannah's husband loved her dearly and proved it when it was time to sacrifice. He gave to his other wife and their children a portion, but to Hannah he gave a bigger portion. He did not hold it against her that she could not have children.

Year after year, Hannah went through this pain with Peninnah. Peninnah was not focused on the worship but used the time to remind Hannah that she was less than Peninnah. Hannah wept, and it hurt her husband. He was saddened that she would not eat and that her heart was grieved. He tried to assure her that he loved her more than ten sons. Nevertheless, she still prayed and asked God for a son. Her pain was so deep that even the priest thought she was drunk when she was truly praying. Once she declared her loyalty to God, the priest told her to go home, and God would open her womb. And God did!

Hannah rejoiced in the power of the Lord to meet every need and elevate her above her circumstances. She followed her prayer with praise to thank God for breaking down the works of the enemy against her. Hannah understood that it was the Lord who brings us up from our low places. In humility, she let God know she recognized that the world belongs to him and he could move as he pleased. We must be careful to always give thanks when we have received our request (see 1 Samuel chapters 1 and 2).

When it rains we must continue to pray. Sometimes our hurt is so great that we don't have the words to really pray, but here Hannah wept. We may have to cry our way through prayer, but we must pray. Had Hannah refused to pray during the time of worship, she would not have received her request. Hannah did not fail, year after year, to continue to worship, to let God know that she still loved him and believed that he was able to meet her need.

It is a trick of the enemy to try to separate us from God. He wants to steal our relationship with God. That is why he was kicked out of heaven. He wanted to *be* God and be worshiped. When he hit the earth, he still had not learned his lesson. He set out in the garden to separate Adam from his relationship with God. His intentions have not changed. He is still trying to take us from God, but the Lord says, "If my people, which are called by name, shall humble themselves, and pray, and seek my face, and turn from their wicked ways; then will I hear from heaven, and will forgive their sin, and will heal their land" (2 Chronicles 7:14). We must commit ourselves to prayer when we are in the rain. Prayer will keep our connection with God and will help us to focus on Him and not on our situation. When we pray, we are sure to hear from God.

RISE AND GO UP FROM HERE

Every storm is an opportunity to rise

to another level.

The best example we have in the Bible is Jesus! He overcame rain in his life on earth, and he overcame the most intense storm of all – being crucified. His life and journey to death resulted in his rising. Like Jesus, we must be willing to go through the same suffering, dying, and rising.

Jesus was sent. He was not here by happenstance. He was not a mistake. He was sent here with a mission to bring man back into fellowship with God. We too have an assignment and a purpose. We can take comfort that we are in good company. God says, "Before I formed thee in the belly I knew thee; and before thou camest forth out of the womb I sanctified thee, *and* I ordained thee a prophet unto the nations" (Jeremiah 1:5).

Jesus was born in a manger, not a beautiful birthing suite or bed and breakfast. Mary "brought forth her firstborn son, and wrapped him in swaddling clothes, and laid him in a manger; because there was not room for them in the inn" (Luke 2:7). Our Lord in flesh was born among animals and placed in a trough the cattle used to eat from. I cannot help but wonder that if they had known who he was, would they have made room for him or even given up their own room?

It doesn't matter where you come from or where you first laid your head. God is not a respecter of persons, and that means he is available to everyone. It isn't contingent on your earthly lineage, but he is accessible because of your royal spiritual lineage. Though the son of God was laid in a manger, it was not the end of his story. It was not his destiny to remain there.

We cannot allow our bloodlines or geographical location to limit what God has for us. It cannot be an excuse to wallow when we fail or accept defeat when we are down. Jesus knew what the innkeepers did not realize. He was royalty. And so are we. Those who cannot recognize it are not our problem. We should not spend our time trying to convince them otherwise.

Jesus fasted. He was tempted in the wilderness. Jesus was preparing himself for the journey ahead. He demonstrated the importance of fasting. The disciples attempted to heal a mute boy of an evil spirit that would not let him talk. It would throw the boy to ground, "and he foameth, and gnasheth with his teeth, and pineth away" (Mark 9:18). The boy's father brought him to the disciples, but they could not cast out the spirit. Jesus commanded the spirit to leave the boy and it did. When the disciples asked Jesus why they couldn't cast out the spirit, He said, "This kind can come forth by nothing, but by prayer and fasting" (Mark 9:29). The disciples could not cast out this spirit because they had not been fasting and praying. Their commands were of no effect.

After Jesus fasted for forty days and forty nights, the devil appeared to tempt him. He expected Jesus to be either weak and off-guard or euphoric with victory. Like Jesus, we must push back our plates as a means of crucifying our flesh. When we deny ourselves of the carnal things, our spirits become more sensitive to God. When we fast, we are telling our bodies that they do not have control over our actions. We are also positioning ourselves for victories that otherwise are unattainable. And, like Jesus, we all will face temptation in the wilderness. What is the wilderness? It is the place where we are surrounded by circumstance and cannot find our way. We wander aimlessly, wishing we could see the clearing, but we only must let God guide us out of the wilderness.

Jesus was betrayed by one that he had done so much for (see Matthew 26:25). This is not unfamiliar ground for us either. We can be betrayed by those closest to us, and it is a heavy rain. Judas shared bread with Jesus and had access to all that Jesus touched. It wasn't enough for him. Judas' focus wasn't on his relationship, but on what he could get. After the kiss, he realized too late that he betrayed a man that did nothing but love him. Like Jesus, we too will experience the pain of betrayal, but we have to keep going.

Jesus was greeted with adoration and sentenced to death all in a week's time. It did not take long for the tides to turn. We have people in our corner who say that they are for us and with us but can change up quickly. It is a false sense of loyalty, sometimes based on the popular vote. Jesus was not fooled by their actions. He cannot be tricked into a false sense of security because he is secure! Our security isn't in ourselves but should rest solely on the Father, the Son, and the Holy Ghost. We must be able to endure the turn of man in favor of the consistency of our God.

Jesus was bound and taken away. After Jesus was betrayed with a kiss, his captors restrained him (see Matthew 26:50). Like Jesus, we too can be bound by people's fear, our pain, disappointments, and loss. Do we hold fast to our convictions? Do we make a decision to keep going, keep believing, and keep trusting God? Or do we allow the rain to simply take us away? How does the rain do that? When we become sad and depressed, it spills into our everyday interactions with God, our families, and our surroundings. We don't really notice it because we are so caught up with the rain. Eventually, we can find ourselves alone and lost. Like Jesus, we must remain on the path God has set before us. We cannot give up.

Jesus was abandoned. Peter was adamant that he would not forsake Jesus, but Jesus, knowing the truth, rebuked him. Peter believed that nothing would separate them. The disciples loved Jesus but became afraid when he was taken away. Though they were *disciples*, they did not remain with Jesus when it mattered most. In fact, Peter denied Jesus: "I do not know the man" (Matthew 26:72). To further prove he was not a follower, Peter changed his character and his manner of speaking: "Then began he to curse and to swear, saying I know not the man" (Matthew 26:74).

Sometimes we have people in our lives that we would never believe would leave us. We boldly state our confidence in them without realizing that God has a plan for everyone – not just us. Often, the plans are not the same. Like Jesus, we must realize that parting is necessary for various reasons. Either we have become so dependent on one another that we have allowed the other to map our path instead of God, or we have simply run our course together and it is time to move in different directions. Separation is not always because there is strife or a falling out, but because we grew apart and the time drew nigh to part ways. Peter could not go the whole journey with Jesus. He had to separate. This solidified what Christ had shared and made Peter realize his own vulnerabilities.

Jesus suffered. He was taunted and told that if he was indeed the King of the Israel then he should save himself (see Matthew 27:42). He did not let the suffering deter him, change his character, or stop his assignment. It was prophesied in the Old Testament how Jesus would be beaten, pierced in the side, and nailed to the cross. He knew he would be mocked as he did the work of God and even as he hung on the cross. Like Jesus, we too will suffer. We will have trials, tribulations, and pain. Like Jesus, we too will be mocked for our commitment to God. Though he could have come down from the cross, he remained and continued to suffer. His goal was to fulfill his assignment. We also must stay the path that we may accomplish our assignment.

Jesus was crucified and died. Jesus could have come down from the cross and proven that he is the King of Kings. He could have literally thrown his weight around. The earthquake could have been his exacting justice on those that were trying to kill him. Instead, he remained focused on his assignment and the outcome of that assignment. He was on the cross to take on our sins and he died to redeem us. We would have been lost if he had decided to use his muscle and, let's be clear, he had every right to do so. He was wrongly accused and convicted. His ego was not at stake. He had *nothing* to prove.

Like Jesus, we will experience a spiritual crucifixion and, for some, a natural death. This is the time that people have turned against us or that our situation has begun to kill our hopes and our dreams. It is also something we must be willing to endure. We must also be willing to die to our flesh. The flesh is hungry and thirsty for self-satisfaction, just as our souls are hungry and thirsty for God. Denying our flesh will feed our souls and strengthen us. What are we willing to give up? What's more important? We don't have to get revenge or make people pay. We don't have to prove that we are stronger, smarter, or more deserving. We only have to present our bodies a living sacrifice and prove what is that good, and acceptable, and perfect, will of God (see Romans 12:1-2).

Jesus ascended. Jesus went through hell before he was resurrected and ascended. How can we ascend and what does that really mean for us? It means that we have to go through the rain in our lives to rise with the victory. Every storm provides the opportunity to rise to another level with God. When our strength in him is increased, we rise spiritually. The genius of God is that we don't have to wait until it's over to rise. We can rise and have victory *in* our situation. We have the victory when we refuse to give up. When we fall and get back on track, we rise. When we withstand betrayal, limitations, abandonment, and suffering, we ascend. Like with Jesus, God gets the glory.

CHAPTER 7
AFTER THE RAIN

The rain has stopped, have you?

No matter what state you are in, you must learn how to go forward after your rain. You must realize that coming out of the rain extends beyond deliverance from the situation. The change in your surroundings is not enough. You need change within, and that change is wholeness. Seek his wholeness more than just freedom. God wants to touch the circumstance of your spirit.

Jesus, his disciples, and a great multitude were leaving Jericho when they passed by a blind man, named Bartimaeus, begging on the highway. He heard Jesus coming through with a great crowd. "He began to cry out, and say, Jesus, *thou* son of David, have mercy on me" (Mark 10:47). The disciples were disturbed by his clamoring, but he just got louder. You cannot let people try to hush you when you *know* Jesus is in the room and you *know* what you need. Though they could see his impairment, they could not see his heart. Surely after living with blindness, he had many feelings and emotions relating to what he had experienced and how he was treated. He no doubt had some esteem issues that needed to be addressed. Whether he knew it or not, he was asking for more than just sight. He wanted to see all of himself.

Jesus stopped walking and called for Bartimaeus to be brought to him. His words were not those of rebuke but of comfort. Jesus said, "What wilt thou that I should do unto thee? The blind man said unto him, Lord, that I might receive my sight. And Jesus said unto him, Go thy way; thy faith hath made thee whole. And immediately he received his sight, and followed Jesus in the way" (Mark 10:51-52). It is so important to pay attention to the question Jesus asked. Surely, Jesus already knew what the man needed but he asked what he wanted. We can be set free – when we want it. Bartimaeus answered and Jesus spoke the word. He did not realize that Jesus could touch more than his eyes. Jesus gave him vision *and* new life. When he could see, he followed Jesus. That is where your wholeness begins; when you follow the face of God and not stop at his hand.

I liken wholeness to a heart attack. When one has a heart attack, the whole body is affected; particularly, blood pressure, breathing, and mobility. When the attack is over, the doctor examines the full body. There are instructions given to prevent another attack. Lifestyle changes, such as diet, exercise, and relaxation, are suggested to strengthen the heart and improve the body's future. The same holds true when God delivers you. The condition and the symptoms are addressed and now the mind, body, and spirit must be primed for a better future. Wholeness is the full body engaged in relationship with God. Come out of your storm, loving him more, giving him more, and following him closer!

When Jesus brings you out, it is his desire that you are not only unbroken but changed. The storms in your life do not have to break you, but they do have to change you – for the better. If you are not changed for the better, ask yourself if you have accepted wholeness. God is still working on your behalf, but your will must give deference to his will. You must want for yourself what God wants for you. Without your openness to be different, change is not accomplished.

I've heard it said that people sin because God has not delivered them yet. Is it possible that they have yet to walk in what was already done for them on the cross? If we believe (and I do) that God sees us as we *will be*, then how can we be waiting on *his* deliverance? Has it not already come? If we believe it has (and I do) then we must also believe that we have to take some action on our own behalf. Not that we can save ourselves, but *we can* ready our souls. Let us "lay aside every weight, and the sin which doth so easily beset *us*, and let us run with patience the race that is set before us, looking unto Jesus the author and finisher of *our* faith; who for the joy that was set before him endured the cross, despising the shame, and is set down at the right hand of the throne of God" (Hebrews 12:1-2).

When you are delivered from sin, you are to sin no more. Look at the man at the pool of Bethesda. There was a healing pool by the sheep market where many sick people lay waiting for the season when the angel would stir the water. Those who stepped in the water first would be healed. Among the sick was a man who had been paralyzed for thirty-eight years. Jesus said to him, "Wilt thou be made whole? The impotent man answered him, Sir, I have no man, when the water is troubled, to put me into the pool: but while I am coming, another steppeth down before me. Jesus saith unto him, Rise, take up thy bed, and walk. And immediately the man was made whole, and took up his bed and walked: and on the same day was the sabbath... Afterward Jesus findeth him in the temple, and said unto him, Behold, thou art made whole: sin no more, lest a worse thing come unto thee" (John 5:6-9, 14). The man was given a charge to sin no more. Jesus pointed out that he was now whole and had to take some responsibility to remain that way. When you fail to accept the charge you are given to follow Christ and sin no more, you expose yourself to not only returning to your former state, but an even worse condition.

"Be strong in the Lord and the power of his might" (Ephesian 6:10). *Be* is an action verb. To complete the directive here, you must be intentional in thought. You have to take more responsibility in your salvation. Christ took action on your behalf and you must respond with action. Denying your flesh must be an act of crucifixion for the devil and resurrection for you. This requires you to change your way of thinking. Back to the heart attack analogy. Before a person makes a lifestyle change, first he must recognize it is needed. To do that, the mind has to accept the need. To be successful, the mind must reject any thoughts that oppose the objective. In order words, if he does not think he needs to change his diet, then he will not do so. If you make a change without believing it is really necessary, then it will not stick. That change will only be temporary until you take it as seriously as life and death. It *is* that serious.

Remember that God's love is everlasting and that he chastens whom he loves so that he will be purified. When we consider everlasting in biblical terms we usually think of the hereafter. Accepting Jesus as the son of God and all that he has done for you on the cross, gives you access to eternal life. Before, you lived as dead men walking, a sinner destined for hell, but coming to know Jesus, you pass from death to life through salvation. It is a great comfort to know that you will spend eternity with God one day. But what about now? Everlasting also means to be carried throughout your life. Be assured that God is here with you through every storm in your life.

The devil will of course try to convince you that when the rain fell, God left your side and left you to fend for yourself. This kind of thinking can make you feel weak and vulnerable. Resist it, and remind the devil that it is written: "When thou art in tribulation, and all these things are come upon thee, *even* in the latter days, if thou turn to the LORD thy God, and shalt be obedient unto his voice; (For the LORD thy God *is* a merciful God;) he will not forsake thee, neither destroy thee, nor forget the covenant of thy fathers which he sware unto them" (Deuteronomy 4:30-31).

It is written, "Thou wilt keep *him* in perfect peace, *whose* mind *is* stayed *on thee*; because he trusteth in thee. Trust ye in the LORD for ever: for in the LORD JEHOVAH *is* everlasting strength" (Isaiah 26:3-4).

Your strength and hope do not lie in you, but in your God, who is strong and mighty. His strength does not fail so he has a never-ending supply to share with you. He never runs out of peace, hope, or protection. You are his child and he delights to share with you, just as he shared all he formed with Adam. The psalmist declared that he who lives in "the secret place of the most High shall abide under the shadow of the Almighty" (Psalm 91:1). The shadow speaks to the understanding of divine alignment. God is bigger than you and your problems, and you must profess he is *your* refuge and fortress. He is the safest place you can dwell, therefore trust he is able to take care of you in your storm. The author of Psalm 91 (attributed to Moses or David) wrote that God:

> shall cover thee with his feathers, and under his wings shalt thou trust: his truth *shall be thy* shield and buckler. Thou shalt not be afraid for the terror by night; *nor* for the arrow *that* flieth by day; *Nor* for the pestilence *that* walketh in darkness; *nor* for the destruction *that* wasteth at noonday. A thousand shall fall at thy side, and ten thousand at thy right hand; *but* it shall not come nigh thee. There shall no evil befall thee, neither shall any plague come nigh thy dwelling.

Thou shalt tread upon the lion and adder: the young lion and the dragon shalt thou trample under feet. Because he hath set his love upon me, therefore will I deliver him: I will set him on high, because he hath known my name. He shall call upon me, and I will answer him: I *will be* with him in trouble; I will deliver him, and honour him. With long life will I satisfy him, and shew him my salvation (Psalm 91:4-7,10,13-16).

Both Moses and David have reason and experience enough to understand the protection of God during trials. Moses best learned of his strength when he was commissioned to confront Pharaoh with releasing God's people. Pharaoh refused but only temporarily. When he released them, he pursued them all the way to the Red Sea, no doubt thinking he had the upper hand. God showed his love and protection when he instructed Moses to stretch out his rod and the waters parted. The children of Israel crossed over on dry land. Pharaoh continued to chase them and was drowned when God closed the water.

David boasted of the power of God and his ability to take down the enemy. He learned to hide himself behind God rather than before him. David's confidence and love for God was his saving grace. He also knew intimately of God's protection. Because of his great success as a warrior and gaining the admiration of the people, Saul sought to kill David. The priests cared for David by providing both natural and spiritual sustenance. They consulted God for David and David, though in danger, was given victory in the battle to save Keilah (see 1 Samuel chapter 23). You too have the same victory over your enemies and the same protection over your home.

It is imperative that you continue to examine your rain. There are a few questions that will better help you understand what you are dealing with at this time in your life:

- How did I get here?
- What were the factors that brought me to this place?
- What is the purpose of my rain?
- Am I experiencing rain that I created?
- What changes do I need to make to prevent self-inflicted rain from happening again?
- What can I do to embrace what God is doing in my life?

- What specific actions can I take now?
- How can I be made whole?
- How will I celebrate God's purpose of my rain?
- How can I help my neighbor?

You may be in a place of wilderness right now and wonder how you will ever get to a clearing. Take heed to what God has spoken to you throughout this book. Lay hold to the principles of your salvation. God sent his son Jesus to bring you into relationship with him. That bond is one of love, grace, mercy, forgiveness, and purpose.

Be encouraged and know that your rain shall pass. You will not be in this place forever. Joyous days are now! Happiness is based on our circumstances, while joy is internal. Your joy doesn't come from where you are, but from whose you are. When the rain comes, don't despair. You can look to him. You have seen that God is your ruler and redeemer and he is in control of all things. He directs your paths and leads you through storms to produce refreshing, growth, restoration, correction, and renewal. In the storms, lean on him and find your way. Allow the rain to nourish you and drive you to the shelter of God. Remember that this is not all that God has for you.

You have the ability to strengthen your bond with God when you decide to embrace your pain and celebrate God's purpose for you. Be an active participant in your healing, deliverance, and miracles. The eyes of your heart have been opened. Go forward with God.

AFTERWORD

The transfiguration of Jesus took place on a mountain top (see Matthew 17:1-9). It is at that moment when Jesus' appearance changed from natural to spiritual. Matthew speaks of his face as shining like the sun and his clothes white as light. Luke described the scene as the glory of Jesus. When we are seen as Jesus was to the disciples, the glow of God will be all over us. We will shine as pure gold when we have been tried in the fire. Rain can change our spiritual state if we allow it.

Heavenly Father, thank you for being my God. You are holy and there is none like you. Thank you for loving me so deeply that you sent your son Jesus for me. I believe you have ordained the words of this book to strengthen and encourage me. Lord, help my heart to embrace what you are doing in my life. Deal with my emotions, my pain, and my weariness. God, show me how to use the rain for your glory and please let it produce fruit in my spirit, my soul, my life, and my environment. Thank you for speaking to me. I am listening. In Jesus' name, amen.

My rain makes me shine. His reign

makes me rise! #Dr. Dee™

ABOUT THE AUTHOR

Evangelist Dr. Delon Radebaugh believes in the sovereignty of God, and the power of his word! As a direct result of God proving Himself to her in dark times, she shares a message of hope and encouragement. She strives to inspire nations to love themselves as the Lord designed them and to love the Lord as he commanded them.

She is the founder of Exceeding Abundantly Ministries where she ministers through evangelism, youth workshops, women's conferences, music, books, and the preached infallible word of God. She is also the Founder and Author of SheVictory, a blog dedicated to inspiring and uplifting the women of God. She is the author of five published books: *A Little Girl's Journey: I made it! The Storyteller's Work In Progress, Learning to Love Me More, Created In His Image: I Am Divine, and Yes, I Can! 30 Days of Real Talk Encouragement.*

Dr. Radebaugh earned her Master's and Doctorate degrees in Theology, with an emphasis in Christian Counseling, from Northwestern Seminary of Theology in 2014.

Since 1993, she has served at her local church, Unity Pentecostal Temple Church of God in Christ, in Denver, Colorado, under the leadership of Pastor Odie Kennedy.

Best of all, Evangelist Dr. Delon Radebaugh is the wife of Deacon Keith Radebaugh and mother of four amazing children, Jarred, Jordan, Jonah, and Hannah, one daughter-in-love, Malorie, and two handsome grandsons, Luca and Logan. They are her first ministry!

God has called Evangelist Radebaugh to encourage souls to enter relationship with HIM, and to inspire all to be strengthened, healed and empowered. She fully embraces the mission of her late Superintendent, Pastor Lamar Kennedy, "Reaching the Lost At Any Cost!"

Stay connected
Follow on Twitter: @DelonRadebaugh
Follow on Facebook: Dr. Delon Radebaugh

Follow on Instagram: @drdeewrites
www.shevictory.com
www.drdelonradebaugh.com

Follow Addison Aitch on Twitter @alphawolfsports
Facebook: Alpha Wolf Sports
www.alphawolfsports.blogspot.com

Connect with Sharndell Lowe on Instagram @cupcakeandasmile
Facebook: Cupcake and a Smile, LLC
www.cupcakeandasmile.com

CPSIA information can be obtained
at www.ICGtesting.com
Printed in the USA
BVHW04s1558160918
527626BV00004B/4/P

9 781644 381878